W9-CGO-338

MANAGING
CREATIVITY
The Innovative Research Library

Ronald C. Jantz

Association of College and Research Libraries
A division of the American Library Association
Chicago, Illinois 2016

The paper used in this publication meets the minimum requirements of American National Standard for Information Sciences–Permanence of Paper for Printed Library Materials, ANSI Z39.48-1992. ∞

Library of Congress Cataloging-in-Publication Data

Names: Jantz, Ronald C., author.
Title: Managing creativity : the innovative research library / Ronald C.
  Jantz.
Description: Chicago : Association of College and Research Libraries, a
  division of the American Library Association, 2016. | Series: Publications
  in librarianship ; no. 70 | Includes bibliographical references.
Identifiers: LCCN 2016004615| ISBN 9780838988343 (pbk. : alk. paper) | ISBN
  9780838988350 (pdf) | ISBN 9780838988367 (epub) | ISBN 9780838988374
  (kindle)
Subjects: LCSH: Research libraries--Administration. | Academic
  libraries--Administration. | Research libraries--Technological
  innovations. | Academic libraries--Technological innovations. |
  Organizational change. | Libraries and colleges--United States.
Classification: LCC Z675.R45 J36 2016 | DDC 025.1/97--dc23 LC record available at
  http://lccn.loc.gov/2016004615

Printed in the United States of America.

20 19 18 17 16 5 4 3 2 1

Contents

Foreword

I HAVE NOTICED OVER the last several years that my presentations at professional meetings have become more alarmist and strident. I have subscribed to the Emerson adage that sometimes a scream is better than a thesis. Ronald Jantz's excellent analysis, building on his doctoral dissertation at Rutgers University, of new models for innovation in the North American research library regrounds me, focusing attention on the theories and research literature of innovation. The study presents a rich and rigorous analysis of the environmental, organizational, and individual characteristics that promote innovation. And it provides a thoughtful look at future research needs and the prospects for innovation in the research library.

Research libraries, in particular the members of the Association of Research Libraries, have over the decades been a frequent subject of investigation. These libraries, rightly or wrongly, have been viewed as bellwether organizations, as indicators of trends and leadership that influence the wider higher education and library communities. These libraries have entered a period of gross mutability, a state of constant change, of productive and powerful chaos, of hybrid strategies and maverick structures, of radical shifts in professional staffing, of massive leadership turnover, and of essential creativity in advancing individual and collective visions. The 21st-century academic research library must be driven by innovation; a focus on redefining the physical (where), expertise (who), and intellectual (why) infrastructure; and an understanding of the psychology, economics, and methods of progress.

The library has always been a fundamental partner in the learning and research processes. But key changes in the information, technology, economic, social, and political environments are challenging this relationship and raising critical questions about the value and impact of the library in the university. Do 20th-century skills still matter? The work of information selection, acquisition, and synthesis: the support provided for navigation, dissemination, interpretation, and understanding; the tools for use, application, and archiving of information... does the research community still need this support in the ways that libraries have provided it over the last 50 years? And do the new roles that research libraries are advancing as aggressive consumers, intermediaries, and aggregators; publishers and educators; research and development organizations; creative and maker spaces, entrepreneurs, and policy advocates... do these present a refreshed opportunity for innovation and for library centrality in the university?

In the context of persistent and evolving roles for the research library, what Ron Jantz refers to as an ambidextrous orientation, the research library will be viewed in increasingly expansive and schizophrenic ways. The library will be legacy, responsible for centuries of societal records in all formats. It will be infrastructure, the essential combination of space, technology, systems, and expertise. It will be repository, ensuring the long-term availability and usability for intellectual and cultural output, increasingly born digital. It will be portal, serving as a sophisticated and intelligent gateway to expanding multimedia and interactive content and tools. It will be enterprise, much more concerned about innovation, business planning, competition, and risk. And it will be public interest, defending and advancing information policy in the public interest. These perspectives suggest that the library will be virtual, engaged with users in ever more rigorous and effective ways. It will be virtuoso, smart but ready to learn, expert but also compassionate. It will be virtuous, radically collaborative, and always working in the interest of students and researchers. It is in this context that innovation must advance.

Cooperation is part of the professional DNA of research libraries, and innovation must increasingly be viewed not just at the local level, but in the context of new collaborations and national and global systemic strategies. From the conditions of knowledge scarcity over the centuries to the oppression of information overabundance in today's and tomorrow's research library, cooperation has been and will be a constant for service, success, and survival. The definition and view of the research library as an independent and self-sustaining organization, collaborating and sharing resources on the margin, has persisted. The future health of the research library will be increasingly defined by new and energetic relationships and combinations and in innovative entrepreneurial partnerships. Radical collaboration encourages fresh thinking about mass production operations, about centers of excellence, deep and shared polycentric strategies for specialized expertise and service, new infrastructures and platforms, and new initiatives, programs, and projects based on shared investment in experimentation. The measures of success for collaboration must be quality, productivity, leadership, and innovation. Are we producing something new, saving resources, and achieving something better together than working alone?

Jantz provokes us to think about how innovation occurs in complex social organizations. In the current period of polygamy, with rampant partnering and combinations; in the coming period of parabiosis, with deep pairings of libraries; and in the future period of particularism, with powerful disciplinary, service, technology, and workflow specializations across the research library communities, the context and challenges of innovation will need to be extrapolated. Jantz provides us with the theory, analysis, and impetus to think about research libraries in new ways.

To achieve the culture of innovation that Jantz encourages, the research library must reach beyond strategic planning exercises and embrace strategic thinking and action to drive decisions and choices. The existing structures and processes are built for a slower pace of change, and planning is often not linked to university priorities. Resource allocations are not guided by strategies, as the library budget is often the best definition of organizational commitments. And planning cycles are often fiscal year–based, rather than ongoing and strategic.

Jantz demonstrates the important link between organizational culture and structure and the presence and success of innovation. Research libraries must dismantle traditional hierarchical and bureaucratic models to create more agile advancement and more robust internal and external communications. The basis of any organization is individuals and groups carrying out roles and working together to achieve shared objectives with a formal structure and with set processes. Organizations define the systems through which priorities are established, decisions are made, resources are allocated, power is wielded and shared, plans are accomplished, and innovation is embraced. Libraries have struggled to distribute authority, integrate operations, break down ineffective workflows, achieve less rigidity, and promote more open consultation and cooperation. We are seeing more and more structures that lend themselves to innovation, with centralized planning and resource allocation and administrative systems coexisting with broadly distributed and loosely coupled structure and an expanding array of maverick units like research centers and entrepreneurial enterprises. Fresh thinking about organization will encourage renewed transformation: changes in composition and structure (what we are and what we do), in outward form and appearance (how we are viewed and understood), and in character and condition (how we do it).

Jantz draws a clear line between innovation and the people who work in and lead the research library. There is a pressing need to confront the human resource and staffing challenges and build new approaches to professional preparation, advancement, and leadership. There are several aspects of 21st-century academic library staffing that are aligned with the ability to be innovative. Research libraries must articulate a broadly understood and accepted vision of librarianship, a new professional paradigm that incorporates strategic visions and qualities. A viable workforce plan has not been developed for research libraries, defining and projecting personnel requirements in terms of quantity and quality. The library education programs are not graduating librarians in sufficient numbers to provide the essential leadership, and those that do graduate are not critical of current structures, current programs, and even the information value systems. Research libraries are not responding effectively to the demographic shifts that are expanding cultural, racial, and ethnic diversity. Staff development has not been viewed as an integral and essential component of organizational success, with continuing education and even certification based on assessment of needs, recognized and well-supported in budget planning, and mandated for all employees. All professional staff, increasingly diffusive in terms of academic credentials and career paths, must have a clear sense of personal mission (why am I in this field?), a self-vision (what do I want to accomplish?), a strong base of knowledge and expertise, strategic positioning (what is my career path?), a strong professional voice, and a commitment to continuous improvement.

In the fall of 2013, the Association of Research Libraries launched a strategic thinking and design process using the next 20 years as a timeframe to predict long-term changes and an evolutionary path for research libraries. The framework sees research libraries as active across institutional boundaries. Research libraries will be an augmented information lens for engaging and empowering individuals, an open symposium for facilitating exploration and exchange within an academic community, a meta-library ecosystem for powerful collaborative capacity, and a knowledge trust for providing enduring, barrier-free access for all research inquiry. ARL embraced a system of action: the collective collection, deep and wide platforms for ensuring knowledge resources are available; scholarly dissemination engines, promoting wide-reaching and sustainable communication of research; libraries that learn, with integrated analytical environments and tools to mine data for transformation; the ARL academy, fostering and nurturing creative, effective, and diverse research library leadership; an innovation lab, incubator for new ideas and the seeds of change. This plan also identifies essential capacities that support this direction for research libraries: advocacy and policy, assessment, communication and marketing, and partnerships.

The ARL plan, for me, defines the what of research library innovation. Ronald Jantz's thinking and research helps us to understand the how. He probes the factors that influence innovation, helping us to review the relevant theory and scholarship, mapping information from the for-profit sector to an understanding of the institutional nonprofit. He produces an extraordinary database of information about the research library community and the impact of global, institutional, and individual characteristics on effective change. It is a masterful analysis that is strong in its methodology but so understandable in its presentation. He looks in particular at integrated leadership, effective decision-making, and flexibility as key defining factors. And he identifies key barriers to innovation and thoughtful strategies for creating a more aggressive and successful path to innovation in the research library.

James G. Neal
University Librarian Emeritus
Columbia University

Preface

THIS BOOK IS ABOUT understanding how research libraries can become more innovative. The major objective is to explain the many possible factors that govern organizational innovation and demonstrate how these factors affect innovation in a unique nonprofit institution—the university research library. The need for institutional leaders to understand and manage innovation cannot be overstated. Strategy, organizational structure, the external environment, and the management of people all loom large as both obstacles and opportunities. In this text, theory, research, and an empirical study of research libraries are all used to inform readers about the complex process of innovation and organizational change. As such, this text builds on the many years of accumulated knowledge and research by prominent scholars who have studied organizational change and innovation. The challenge for this author is to locate innovation research within the context of the institutional nonprofit and to clarify where prior research, primarily focused on the for-profit sector, can also provide insight into how the library innovates.

The research library offers a fascinating and contradictory world. In his inspiring and eloquent monograph simply entitled *Library*, Battles (2003, 4) captures some of the enduring images of the research library:

> In the library, the reader is wakened from the dream of
> communion with a single book, startled into recognition
> of the word's materiality by the sheer number of bound
> volumes; by the sound of pages turning; covers rubbing;
> by the rank smell of books gathered together in vast
> numbers.

In a sense, this quotation helps explain the challenge for today's library leaders. How are they to preserve and maintain the image and value of the traditional library while also undertaking the seemingly mandatory changes that will be necessary to meet the information needs of our 21st-century society?

John Budd has written extensively about academic libraries and librarians, urging them to undertake a more critical examination of the underlying purposes of their profession—"it is the judgment—the reflective judgment—that both sets our profession apart from others and forms the basis of our principal responsibility" (2008, 88). As part of this self-reflection, an important question is likely to emerge. Is an innovative library culture essential for the research library future, and, if so, how is this culture to be realized? Although culture can constrain our actions, it can also be a vehicle for change. It is this dilemma that has provided the motivation for the author to take up the study of innovation in research libraries.[1]

Overview of Organization and Chapters

This book on ARL library innovation is comprised of three parts. The first part, consisting of chapters one through three, begins by taking a historical perspective of some 100 years of library innovations and how these innovations are related to events both within and external to the library. The examples in chapter one provide a transition to chapters two and three and the discussion of important concepts in the innovation research literature.

In chapter one, the difficulty of organizational change in the library is illustrated by citing examples of innovation, beginning in the late 19th century. These examples are linked to concepts in the innovation literature that have been shown to affect the innovativeness of an organization. Chapter two introduces organizational innovation and highlights the unique aspects of the research library that faces challenges, not only from the broader external environment but also from its own parent institution. In chapter three, the fundamental innovation process—the dif-

---

[1] This text elaborates on and expands the author's dissertation entitled "Incremental and Radical Innovations in Research Libraries: An Exploratory Examination Regarding the Effects of Ambidexterity, Organizational Structure, Leadership, and Contextual Factors" (see Jantz 2013).

fusion of innovations—is introduced as defined by Rogers (2003, 5–12). Of special note here is that diffusion is a communication process about an idea and typically involves a change in the structure and function of the organization in order to implement a successful innovation. Chapter three expands on the discussion of innovation by reviewing how researchers have articulated the differences between innovation in service organizations, nonprofits, and product or manufacturing firms. An organizational typology is introduced to clarify the differences among the for-profit sector and within the group of nonprofits. The research library is introduced as a member of the class of organizations referred to as institutional nonprofits.

The second part of the book, chapters four through nine, provides an overview of the research model and discusses in detail the results of the empirical analysis of innovation in ARL libraries. Chapter four brings together innovation characteristics, supporting empirical studies, and the research model. In the research model, the independent variables are described along with the unique dependent variable—innovation performance. Chapters five through nine present in detail the major theoretical concepts for the innovation study, review related empirical research, and discuss the significant factors affecting innovation in research libraries that have resulted from the empirical analysis. These factors include the actions of the leadership team, organizational structure, the external environment, and a flexible strategy regarding exploration and support of existing services. For this flexibility, we examine the concept of organizational ambidexterity—the ability of an organization to simultaneously support existing services while also conducting research and developing totally new services. This concept of ambidexterity is one of the most significant in the innovation study and represents a major challenge in the management of an organization that focuses primarily on the quality and reliability of traditional services. In each of these chapters, we will explain the major construct under discussion and the related significance of the statistical findings for the 50 Association of Research Library (ARL) members in the study sample. Of special note, chapter nine discusses library leadership demographics and the surprising and unexpected results from the innovation study.

Part III—chapters ten, eleven, and twelve—explores additional avenues of research that might help us further understand the innovative culture in libraries. In chapter ten, theory and research findings are brought to bear on the practice of managing research libraries, tapping into an emerging area of innovation research that focuses on nontechnical or management innovations. One speculation at this juncture is that management innovations are the primary enablers of major change in the library and are a key to thriving in the future. These innovations are, in a sense, even more important than technical innovations. Management or administrative innovations, originated by library leadership, must precede the technical innovation in order to remove the obstacles that lie in the path to implementation of a major new capability. The examples in this chapter, taken as a whole, represent a research library that is quite different from what exists today. Chapter eleven looks back at the underlying data to expose other meaningful relationships. In this chapter, the impact on innovation of the singular leader and the experience of the for-profit firm are examined, demonstrating the influence of the library director on innovation and suggesting that there is much to learn from corporate experience and practice. Chapter twelve speculates on future possibilities and possible enablers of innovation. The concluding observations suggest that a more philosophical approach might help library leaders create a vision to guide the transformation of the research library.

Who Will Find This Book Useful?

This book is written primarily for academic library leaders, future leaders, managers, and administrators who want to create a culture of innovation in their institutions. Of course, research libraries do innovate today, but there are important distinctions to be noted that could lead to a more innovative culture. For example, seeking knowledge outside of the boundaries of the profession will generate innovative ideas and strengthen the learning orientation of the library. Creating innovation portfolios with a mix of incremental and radical innovations will enable the tracking and management of innovation projects, thereby increasing the probability of successful implementation. Perhaps most importantly for long-term sustainability, leaders can examine the barriers to innovation that have been erected by both the library and the parent institution and look for ways to minimize or remove these barriers.

Although the implications for practice in this text are directed at library leaders, this book also provides an overview of much of the theory and empirical evidence found in the literature of innovation studies. As a result, readers will find the text to be a useful introduction to organizational innovation. Although the literature reviews include research on both service and product organizations, the emphasis in this book is on innovation in the nonprofit sector and, more specifically, what is referred to here as the institutional nonprofit—an organization with well-established professional norms and traditions. Given the theory, literature review, and extensive bibliography, this text could serve quite well as supplementary reading in courses on management in library and information science programs. The practical implications that are discussed in many of the chapters can provide ideas for student projects and assignments.

Finally, this book provides an overview of the research model and empirical findings from the author's PhD dissertation.[2] Researchers in the field of innovation studies have created a variety of models in order to study innovation, frequently focusing on the innovation decision and a limited context. This study examined many aspects of the research library that resulted in 17 possible independent variables. A unique dependent variable, *innovation performance,* was created to capture not only the decision to innovate, but also the extent of implementation and the balance between radical and incremental innovations. As a result, this work contributes to the scholarly research on innovation by applying established theories to a relatively under-studied organizational sector—the institutional nonprofit and the research library.

Empirical Study Sample and Design

The Association of Research Libraries (ARL) is a nonprofit organization of research libraries at comprehensive, research-intensive institutions in the United States and Canada that share similar research missions, aspirations, and achievements. From the population of ARL members in the United States, a sample of 50 libraries was created. For each library, the university librarian and the library leadership team answered survey questions regarding their attitudes toward change, the external environment, the management team, organizational structure, team demographics, and innovations that had been adopted by their institution. Given the data

---

[2] It should be noted that the study supporting the PhD dissertation is referred to frequently in this text as "the ARL study" or "the innovation study."

from survey responses and publicly available data on research libraries, various factors that affect innovation were analyzed. From the hierarchical regression analysis, five factors were shown to have significant associations with innovation performance in the research library.

To Innovation Skeptics

The question that has fascinated me for much of my professional career is "How do groups of people come together to produce something not only truly useful but also a breakthrough that propels users to another level of creativity and productivity?" These successes stand out in the midst of the many necessary improvements required for existing products and the unfortunate failures that will inevitably occur.

Early in my career at Bell Labs, I supervised a group of software engineers who produced one of the first successful interactive graphic systems for the design of printed circuits (Welt 1975). The group was small (five to six members) with complementary skills but with little knowledge of formal software methods that were to be developed much later. Time-shared systems were not as yet well established, so software development was shared on a single Digital Equipment Corporation PDP-15. The graphics display was based on a prototype from the research organization in Bell Labs, representing not only a collaboration between the R&D parts of Bell Labs but also the transfer of technology from research into development (Mancusi and Wild 1972).

Later at Bell Labs, I was fortunate to be a part of a team that was asked to create a totally new communication system for the intermediate-sized business community—what in those days was referred to as a PBX (private branch exchange). This totally new digital system was based on the technologies of microprocessors, software engineering, and VLSI integrated circuits (Feiner, Rodriguez, and Weiss 1985). Three laboratories of hardware, software, and systems engineers dealt with not only apparently intractable technical problems but also the social and human problems of several hundred people working together. In a few short years, Definity System 75 emerged as one of the best-selling products in the business communication marketplace.

In a different social setting, I was also fortunate to be a member of the team in Rutgers University Libraries that created the university's institutional repository—Rutgers University Community Repository (RU-core).[3] Although quite different in purpose, social setting, and underlying technology, there is one striking similarity between these successful initiatives—team members had the freedom and empowerment to think differently and were not constrained by the prevailing culture and conventions.

The innovation naysayers will suggest that these breakthrough products are the result of serendipity—random ideas and processes coming together by chance and resulting in success. It is the challenge of this text to demonstrate, first, that the innovation process can be managed and, second, that the innovations that seem to occur so frequently in both small entrepreneurial businesses and large corporations can also be achieved in an academic institution such as the research library. To address this challenge, the author will need to take the reader into the relevant literature in innovation studies and also bring together the many factors that can affect innovation in the research library. It is expected that the result will be an informative and provocative study, stimulating discussion among library professionals regarding the future of the research library.

Author's Note

Ronald C. Jantz has a BA and an MA in mathematics from the University of Kansas and the University of Michigan, respectively. He worked for many years as a software developer and manager in one of the world's best-known research and development (R&D) organizations—Bell Laboratories. In 1996, he returned to academia and earned a master's degree in library science and a PhD from the School of Communication and Information at Rutgers University. The work presented here brings together his organizational research, the practical experience from managing in an R&D organization, and library experience in which he continues to serve as the Digital Library Architect at Rutgers University Libraries.

Acknowledgments

First and foremost, I want to thank the leaders of the 50 research libraries who agreed to participate in this study of innovation. Many in research

---

[3] RUcore is available at https://rucore.libraries.rutgers.edu.

libraries are plagued with "survey fatigue," and I know the first impulse in a busy library is to say no, especially when three or four members of the leadership team are required to fill out the innovation survey. My spirits were frequently buoyed when these library leaders not only filled out the survey but also wished me luck. Many university librarians voiced interest in the results, and some even discussed the implications of survey questions in their staff meetings. Obviously, I would not have had a dissertation and a published book without the data provided by these library leaders.

As in most significant endeavors, many along the way assist the individual effort, and so it is with my study of innovation. My first library director at Rutgers University Libraries, Ryoko Toyama, provided me with the freedom to prototype and implement software-based applications that demonstrated how a certain amount of individual autonomy can result in new library services. Following this early experience, the encouragement, support, and active engagement of my university librarian, Marianne Gaunt, and my associate university librarian, Grace Agnew, were instrumental not only in suggesting areas to pursue, but also in enabling me to complete the PhD while also working as a librarian at Rutgers University Libraries. In order to get the details right, many Rutgers University librarians, library staff members, and PhD students helped me pretest and debug the innovation survey consisting of 102 questions.

During my seven-year pursuit of the PhD, I was assisted in numerous ways by faculty at the School of Communication and Information. Especially noteworthy, my advisor, Professor Daniel O'Connor, provided much needed guidance regarding statistical methods while also striking, in my mind, a nice advisory balance regarding numerous issues of content and quality. Our mutual interest in research libraries led to many interesting and thought-provoking discussions.

The literature on innovation is vast and difficult for a student to negotiate. Professor Fariborz Damanpour of the Rutgers Business School introduced me to the innovation literature and the unique aspects of organizational innovation. His course, Management of Innovation and Technology, provided not only the inspiration to pursue research in organizational innovation but also the germ of an idea about how the area of innovation studies might be applied to research libraries. I want to also take this opportunity to thank Professor Rebecca Warner of the University of New Hampshire. Of the many books on applied statistics that I have examined in the past several years, her text (2013) on bivariate and multivariate techniques is, without a doubt, the best in explaining the practical, theoretical, and intuitive concepts that are fundamental to regression analysis.

On a personal note, I want to thank my wife, Leona, for her support and love throughout my studies. The pursuit of the PhD and the subsequent book on research library innovation has lasted almost a decade. This endeavor would not have been possible without your patience and unconditional support.

Ronald C. Jantz
Digital Library Architect
Rutgers University Libraries
January 2016

References

Battles, Matthew. 2003. *Library: An Unquiet History.* New York: W. W. Norton & Co.

Budd, John M. 2008. *Self-Examination: The Present and Future of Librarianship.* Westport, CT: Libraries Unlimited.

Feiner, A., E. Rodriguez, and C. Weiss. 1985. "Introduction and Overview." *AT&T Technical Journal: System 75 Digital Communications System* 64, no. 1: 145–47.

Jantz, Ronald C. 2013. "Incremental and Radical Innovations in Research Libraries: An Exploratory Examination Regarding the Effects of Ambidexterity, Organizational Structure, Leadership, and Contextual Factors." Doctoral dissertation, Rutgers University. doi:10.7282/T3ZP44PT.

Mancusi, M. D, and J. C. Wild. 1972. "Interactive Graphics for Schematic Editing, a Working Tool." *Proceedings of the 9th Design Automation Conference,* 301–4. Piscataway, NJ: IEEE Press. doi:10.1145/800153.804961.

Rogers, Everett M. 2003. *Diffusion of Innovations,* 5th ed. New York: Free Press.

Warner, Rebecca M. 2013. *Applied Statistics: From Bivariate through Multivariate Techniques.* Thousand Oaks, CA: Sage.

Welt, Martin J. 1975. "NOMAD: A Printed Wiring Board Layout System." *Proceedings of the 12th Design Automation Conference,* 152–61. Piscataway, NJ: IEEE.

Part One
INNOVATION

Libraries:
Change and Resistance to Change

WHY STUDY INNOVATION IN research libraries? The problem of change in complex social organizations has both theoretical and practical implications. Obstacles and opportunities for change originate within the university and the library and externally in government policy, technological advancements, and population demographics. Library leaders have long articulated the need for change in order for the institution to survive and thrive. However, there is very little research that applies innovation theory to understanding how change occurs in the research library. A primary objective in this study is to apply theory and an empirical analysis to understand organizational change and innovation in the research library in the hope that the results will be beneficial to library practitioners.

Library scholars have commented extensively on the culture of the library that is struggling to move from a bureaucratic model to one that is more dynamic. Noting that progress is a conflict between change and resistance to change, Shera (1971, 64) aptly characterizes the cultural conundrum facing research libraries:

> On the one hand there are the traditionalists, who cling
> close to the solid earth of library convention and shun
> the heights of innovation. They will live to die, not unlike
> Daedalus, the victims of their past achievements, captives
> of a past they helped to create. Against them are arrayed
> the innovators, the intrepid explorers, who reject conven-
> tion as the traditionalists fear the unknown. Their success

is in jeopardy because of failure to profit from the experience of the innovators of an earlier day. In the conflict
between these two groups librarianship suffers.

In similar remarks almost 40 years later, John Budd urges librarians
to overcome conservatism "that preserves past action and thought as in-
herently good" (Budd 2008, 225). In preserving past action, librarians
have evolved highly efficient procedures through many serial, incremental improvements. The more cutting-edge, entrepreneurial initiatives have
progressed slowly, impeded by a bureaucratic organization that is bound
by rules and procedures and is largely subservient to the parent institution. Moving ahead with more radical innovations will require librarians
to think differently, energized by engaged students, faculty collaborators,
and a more supportive organizational climate.

Early Innovations in Research Libraries

The innovation history of the library provides fascinating insight into how
decisions were made to adapt to new technologies and changes in the sur-
roundings of the library over the past 100 years. The emergence of the
modern industrial society, the maturing of the library profession, and the
evolving of the organizational structure have all impacted the ability of
the library to innovate.

The External Environment

Radical change came to the library in the late 19th century with a complete about-face, resulting in a transformation from conservation and
protecting the collection, sometimes chaining books to shelves, to an
emphasis on use—an approach that gradually spread throughout the libraries of Harvard, Columbia, Michigan, and others. Most significant in
this era was the adoption of the German style of graduate education by
Johns Hopkins University (JHU), founded in 1876 as a graduate school
for advanced study. The JHU emphasis resulted in research becoming an
end in itself and a challenge to the primacy of teaching (Atkins 1991, 13–
19). The founding of Johns Hopkins and the appointments of a group of
forceful university leaders resulted in a late-19th-century transformation
of higher education and the academic library.

In some of the early small colonial institutions, the college president was also the librarian. Ravelli (1987) studied the critical forces at play in the libraries of New Jersey's two institutions of higher education with colonial origins—Princeton University and Rutgers University. He reports that Princeton University, under the leadership of President McCosh, established a full-time professional librarian in 1873 with substantial funds for library materials and a separate library building. In the university library, reference service was introduced as one of the more far-reaching innovations (Hamlin 1981, 22–23). At this juncture, Melvil Dewey stepped in to establish the first library school at Columbia University with an emphasis on practical matters, a legacy that still persists in many of today's academic libraries (Atkins 1991, 19).

This emphasis on the user in the library can largely be attributed to the prevailing economic and technological conditions of the late 19th century. From the 1860s to the end of the 19th century, the industrial production of the United States grew to a number one ranking in the world, with inventions such as the typewriter and magnetic tape recording that would ultimately impact library services. Musmann writes that for the first time in history, "the technical capacity of a nation and its ability to compete in the industrial arena became linked to the general education level of the population" (1993, 5–6). These educational demands of a complex industrial society became a major force in reorienting the research library to become a service-providing organization.

Rules and Regulations

Although the progressive view of the world became dominant in the late 19th century, this view did not always result in what might be considered obvious change for the library. In writing about this period, Shera (1972, 262–64) indicates that librarians have frequently been reluctant to adopt new mechanical devices and related technological advances. In preference to using the typewriter for headings on catalog cards, librarians convinced themselves that neatly lettered headings were almost as good and would likely not even be noticed by the casual observer. It seems that a quick adoption of the typewriter would have been an obvious innovation for libraries in the late 1800s. However, from the innovation perspective, two factors were working against the adoption of this new device. First, there was a cultural bias in favor of the skilled practitioner—his or her handwriting was just as good as a typewriter. Secondly, in the modern library of the late 19th century, we were beginning to see the effect of what innovation scholars refer to as "formalism", the preference for rules and procedures and the reluctance to change. These rules provide predictability and help guarantee high-quality service, but they also lead to rigidity and resistance to introducing significant improvements (Hage and Aiken 1970, 21–23). The preference of the librarian hand over the typewriter represents a fundamental cultural pattern within the library in which established rules create obstacles for more innovative approaches. Some 20 years later, the typewriter did become a common appliance in the library, and librarians wanted applicants who knew how to use the machine (Kroeger 1907, 111).

Norms of the Profession

The research of DiMaggio and Powell helps us understand how the norms and traditions of the research library can act as obstacles to change and the generation of new ideas. These researchers state, "Once a set of organizations emerges as a field, a paradox emerges: rational actors make their organizations increasingly similar as they try to change them" (1983, 147). DiMaggio and Powell define three forces of institutional isomorphic change: *coercive*—resulting from both formal and informal pressures exerted from external organizations, *mimetic*—resulting from standard responses to uncertainty, and *normative*—associated with professionalism. As an example, when the library faces uncertainty such as that introduced by the environment and technological advances, a mimetic force can cause imitation where the library adopts services or products that appear to be successful in other similar institutions. This mimetic force produces libraries that are similar in function and operation, frequently a good thing, but also reduces opportunities for more creative approaches.

The normative force acts to retain traditional processes, as when it took decades before librarians were able to accept the photograph as a legitimate part of the library collection. Here we see the norms of the profession acting as an "iron cage" and restricting change in the organization. Librarians had an almost quasi-religious view of the book—"Nothing marks man off from the brute quite as sharply as does the book. Nothing establishes his kinship to God as clearly as does the book" (A. L. Crabb, quoted in Musmann 1993, 16). As in this example, these professional norms reduce variation and block new ideas, resulting in resistance to the more radical innovation.

The Perception of the Innovation

The introduction of the telephone into the library provides a different perspective on a technological innovation that was adopted quickly. In the 1877 annual conference of American Libraries, the president explained the details of how the branches of the Boston Public Library were connected to the central library by means of the telephone. He indicated that it "was remarkably simple and of what great use it would be to libraries having branches in different parts of the city" (President 1877, 22). A few years later, Charles Cutter and John Cotton Dana were on the forefront in proposing unique uses of the telephone, including access to materials in another library and as an interlibrary loan device (Musmann 1993, 126–28).

In making decisions about adopting an innovation, the perceptions of leadership govern the fate of the innovation. Rogers (2003, 219–65) explains how perceived attributes of an innovation can affect the speed with which an innovation is adopted by a social system. For the telephone, three perceived attributes contributed to the rapid adoption and diffusion of this new device in libraries. The *relative advantage* represented a perception that the telephone was superior to earlier forms of communication. The perception of *complexity*, as indicated by the president, was one in which the telephone was viewed as simple and easy to use. *Compatibility* is a perception that the innovation is consistent with existing values. In this case, the telephone represented a totally new technology. However, the ease of use and obvious advantages outweighed concerns that this new device might be incompatible with library culture and practices.

Organizational Structure

The structure of an organization can impact its ability to innovate. From the earliest part of the 20th century, libraries have organized themselves for efficiency and cost-effectiveness, culminating in the two primary functional branches—public services and technical services (Budd 2012, 104). A few top administrators typically hold decision-making authority in this classical library structure. As Hage and Aiken have demonstrated (1970, 38–39), this centralized, top-down approach tends to reduce organizational change and preserve the status quo. The bureaucratic approach structures organizational life by insuring uniformity through the establishment of a set of rules and regulations that are closely followed (Budd 2012, 105). The two concepts of centralization (top-down decision making) and formalism (closely followed rules and regulations), while ostensibly focused on providing a high-quality service, tend to create a culture whose goals are control and efficiency. Together, these factors represent a major obstacle to the library becoming more innovative. Brenda Dervin describes the issue quite succinctly: "The difficulty with structures invented to serve purposes at one point in time is that they live beyond their function. Soon, systems feel constrained to define their functions in terms of available structures, forgetting that structures are inventions" (quoted in Smith 1990, 65).

Incremental Innovations

The traditional environment of the library has been stable and predictable, an organizational context that is highly bureaucratized and leads largely to incremental innovations. These incremental innovations emanate primarily from the librarian-client interface and are focused on improving the quality and reliability of existing services. Melvil Dewey emphasized efficiency and the streamlining of library processes and worked to publicize many ingenious solutions to library problems. These early incremental innovations included various mechanical devices such as pencil sharpeners, typewriters, stamp-affixing machines, and a buzzer for communication in larger buildings (Musmann 1993, 75–76). In fact, early academic librarians were very good at incremental improvements, as can be seen from the continued evolution of reference services from person-to-person communication to the use, today, of e-mail and chat technology. Similarly, university libraries have experimented with outreach and outpost arrangements that place librarians in alternate venues, including student unions, residence halls, and faculty departments, in order to promote information literacy (Kuchi, Mullen, and Tama-Bartels 2004; Rudin 2008). Nadler and Tushman, however, stress the importance of what they call "discontinuous organization change," urging leaders to learn how to manage through periods of both revolutionary and incremental change. In fact, continued incremental change in a dynamic environment is "a recipe for failure" (1990, 94). This perspective argues for a more balanced approach in which research libraries introduce radical innovations along with the many incremental innovations that have been part of the library tradition.

These innovation examples from an earlier era demonstrate the many obstacles that can prevent the implementation of an innovation. Yet research libraries are pushing ahead on new fronts that have promise to become major new services in the university.

Today—Radical Innovations on the Verge of Success

Beginning in the early 1980s, the detrimental effects of the risk-averse library culture became evident in the more negative and ominous tone appearing in the prophecies and predictions of library futurists. Increasingly, these pundits are forecasting the dramatic reduction in library services or the complete disappearance of the library. With potential reductions in services, the library director will have diminished authority and responsibilities, perhaps being reduced to the role of a warehouse coordinator or a study hall administrator (Mash 2010, 19). In Thompson's tract simply entitled "The End of Libraries," he uses a Darwinian analogy suggesting that if libraries do not evolve "they indeed most surely face a dinosaur-type extinction" (1982, 105). Writing about librarians in the age of electronics, Lancaster asserts that "libraries as we know them will become obsolete" and Susan Crooks writes that there is serious concern for the survival of libraries (quoted in Mash 2010, 16–17). More recently, those in the library profession have begun to acknowledge the severity of the problem. Alire and Evans offer a blunt statement: "If libraries do not change, they will join the dinosaurs" (2010, 328). University administrators are beginning to echo these persistent negative views by suggesting that the research library will become primarily a study space, with coffee and special collections (Kolowich 2009). These scholars, librarians, and administrators raise an existential question as to how the library will prevent this slide into irrelevance and oblivion. As in the following two examples, creating totally new service concepts offers an answer to this question.

Research Data Management Services

Almost 10 years ago, data management was identified as an important new service for academic libraries (Carlson 2006). Although library directors appear to support data management as an important service for the institution, recent research suggests that libraries are having difficulty defining and getting started with data management services (Tenopir et al. 2013). In a sample of 100 research libraries, only 15 percent offered the core service of preparing research data for ingest and preservation, whereas 52 percent had no plans for such a service (Tenopir et al. 2014). The most commonly offered data service was one of finding and citing datasets, similar to the traditional reference service, whereas the least commonly offered service involved outreach and collaboration with researchers.

Antell and colleagues (2014) conducted a survey addressed to 507 science librarians regarding participation in data management services. Only 23 percent of 155 respondents felt that they had sufficient skills to take on a data management role, citing unfamiliarity with the data life cycle as a major impediment. Regarding the operation of the data repository, 53.6 percent of 70 respondents were unsure about which campus entity operates the data repository, some suggesting that this function should be under the purview of the university research office. Along with the many other survey responses, this report presents a disturbing picture of uncertainty within the professional librarian ranks and a reluctance to take on this new role of data management.

In a most recent scan of some 35 institutions, most of which are research libraries, Palumbo and colleagues (2015) report that many of these institutions provided research data management consulting and allowed self-deposit of data or self-deposit with mediation. Staffing commitments to launch a comprehensive data service were significant, frequently requiring more than two or three staff members. Responsibility for the protection of confidential data was often placed with the principal investigator, and funding models for storage and preservation varied.

In many respects, the emerging data service represents a quandary for library management in launching new, more radical innovations. The required staff commitment suggests that funds might need to be shifted from traditional services. For the librarian, training requires a much more in-depth engagement in the research process and thorough understanding of the data life cycle, one that can vary significantly across the various disciplines. Although there are obvious technical and policy issues regarding the launching of a data management service, it appears that library directors have been uncertain about proceeding and have not articulated data management as a core service of the library. This lack of a decision reduces commitment among library members and results in confusion regarding the priority of the new initiative relative to more traditional services.

A Geographic Information Systems (GIS) Service

We live in a society of information overload, where new knowledge, spatial relationships, and important data subtleties are hard to come by. Geographic Information Systems (GIS) software offers an approach to revealing these complexities, ones that are almost impossible to represent in a textual or numeric format. GIS applications and related technology are advancing rapidly, seemingly limited only by the imagination. Commercial software vendors are collaborating to integrate open-source tools such as R for spatial analysis. The Environmental Systems Research Institute (ESRI) has previewed a new application that streamlines the processing of image data from drones. GIS applications are transforming scholarship with applications in such diverse areas as exploring Stonehenge landscapes, studying the political impact of the redistricting of electoral units, tracking invasive species, and managing watersheds. Most recently, the World Health Organization used GIS to track the chains of the Ebola virus transmission from one person to another (Wheeler 2015).

Although sophisticated GIS software has been available for well over a decade, research libraries have encountered difficulties in framing a service that offers value to the university and can be accommodated within limited staff resources and budget. Strategic questions must address the relationship of a GIS service to the map print collection and map librarianship. A GIS service would require dedicated staff to master the technology and to provide training and consultation across the three major disciplines—humanities, social sciences, and science. Creation of a geospatial center would likely involve collaboration with academic units that are intensive GIS users, such as geography and public policy. Training and consultation might best be offered by leveraging the expertise of graduate students in these academic units. Creating servers for geospatial data and software would involve the library or university IT organizations. The organizational impact on the library could be significant in the use of new technologies, changes in the liaison relationship, and the alteration of the organizational structure.

The strategic questions are compelling. GIS applications are emerging in every discipline, and students require assistance in order to use GIS software for course projects. Students and faculty are not only searching for data to drive GIS applications, but are also discovering that spatial analysis and visualization represents a most effective method for explaining complex relationships. The library can offer traditional support in terms of research guides and assistance in locating spatial data. Alternatively, the library could create a more comprehensive service, providing GIS workshops, consultation, and convenient access to commercial and open-source software.

Conclusion

In the commercial world, the inability of leaders to divorce themselves from traditions and current products and create totally new business concepts has resulted in the demise of many seemingly invincible corporations. Research libraries are not likely to disappear from the university landscape. However, the creation of new services can reinvigorate the library presence on campus and lead to a reversal in the decline of the past several years.

To innovate at the concept level requires library leaders and members to examine all aspects of the potentially new service. Based on budget constraints and skills, the service might be implemented incrementally. However, a more holistic definition of a new service enables all stakeholders to understand the more comprehensive service trajectory and debate the consequences and benefits of the library embarking on a more radical innovation.

The difficulty in defining totally new services raises the question about how libraries perceive themselves as an organization. The research library is unique in the larger grouping of nonprofit organizations. Although print book collections are no longer doubling every 10 years, libraries are taking on a growing collection of digital projects in which the clients expect the data, documents, maps, media, and photographs will be archived, preserved, and curated in perpetuity. For the research library to energetically engage in exploration, invest in new knowledge and advanced technology, and adapt to the reality of the 21st-century information society, it seems that a new business model is required, one in which new services can be launched with a sense of urgency and an understanding that competition is part of the 21st-century library world. Understanding the fundamentals of an innovative culture will be important for leadership to take the library down this path of more uncertainty and risk.

References

Alire, Camilla A., and G. Edward Evans. 2010. *Academic Librarianship.* New York: Neal-Schuman.

Antell, Karen, Jody Bates Foote, Jaymie Turner, and Brian Shults. 2014. "Dealing with Data: Science Librarians' Participation in Data Management at Association of Research Libraries Institutions." *College and Research Libraries* 75, no. 4: 557–74. doi:10.5860/crl.75.4.557.

Atkins, Stephen E. 1991. *The Academic Library in the American University.* Chicago: American Library Association.

Budd, John M. 2008. *Self-Examination: The Present and Future of Librarianship.* Westport, CT: Libraries Unlimited.

———. 2012. *The Changing Academic Library: Operations, Culture, Environments.* Chicago: Association of College and Research Libraries.

Carlson, Scott. 2006. "Lost in a Sea of Science Data." *Chronicle of Higher Education,* June 23. http://chronicle.com/weekly/v52/i42/42a03501.htm.

DiMaggio, Paul J., and Walter W. Powell. 1983. "The Iron Cage Revisited: Institutional Isomorphism and Collective Rationality in Organizational Fields." *American Sociological Review* 48, no. 2: 147–160.

Hage, Jerald, and Michael Aiken. 1970. *Social Change in Complex Organizations.* New York: Random House.

Hamlin, Arthur T. 1981. *The University Library in the United States: Its Origins and Development.* Philadelphia: University of Pennsylvania Press.

Kolowich, Steve. 2009. "Libraries of the Future." *Inside Higher Ed,* September 24. http://www.insidehighered.com/news/2009/09/24/libraries .

Kroeger, Alice B. 1907. "Instruction in Cataloging in Library Schools." *Library Journal* 32: 108–11.

Kuchi, Triveni, Laura Bowering Mullen, and Stephanie Tama-Bartels. 2004. "Librarians without Borders: Reaching Out to students at a Campus Center." *Reference and User Services Quarterly* 43, no. 4: 310–17. doi:10.7282/T34F1P48.

Mash, S. David. 2010. *Decision Making in the Absence of Certainty: A Study in the Context of Technology and the Construction of the 21st Century Academic Library*. Chicago: Association of College and Research Libraries.

Musmann, Klaus. 1993. *Technological Innovations in Libraries, 1860–1960: An Anecdotal History*. Westport, CT: Greenwood Press.

Nadler, D., and Michael Tushman. 1990. "Beyond the Charismatic Leader: Leadership and Organizational Change." *California Management Review*, 32, no. 2: 77–97.

Palumbo, Laura B., Ron Jantz, Yu-Hung Lin, Aletia Morgan, Minglu Wang, Krista White, Ryan Womack, Yingting Zhang, and Yini Zhu. 2015. "Preparing to Accept Research Data: Creating Guidelines for Librarians." *Journal of eScience Librarianship* 4, no. 2 (November 5). http://escholarship.umassmed.edu/jeslib/vol4/iss2/1.

President. 1877. "Proceedings of Second Annual Conference of American Libraries." *Library Journal* 2: 14–42.

Ravelli, Joseph Louis. 1987. "An Historical Analysis of Academic Library Development in the Late Nineteenth Century: Case Studies of the Libraries of New Jersey's Universities with Colonial Origins: A Dissertation." ProQuest Dissertations & Theses A&I. (303490259).

Rogers, Everett M. 2003. *Diffusion of Innovations*, 5th ed. New York: Free Press.

Rudin, Phyllis. 2008. "No Fixed Address: The Evolution of Outreach Library Services on University Campuses." *Reference Librarian* 49, no. 1: 55–75. doi:10.1080/02763870802103761.

Shera, Jesse Hauk. 1971. *"The Compleat Librarian" and Other Essays*. Cleveland, OH: The Press of Case Western Reserve University.

———. 1972. *The Foundations of Education for Librarianship*. New York: Becker and Hayes.

Smith, Eldred. 1990. *The Librarian, the Scholar, and the Future of the Research Library*. New York: Greenwood Press.

Tenopir, Carol, Robert J. Sandusky, Suzie Allard, and Ben Birch. 2013. "Academic Librarians and Research Data Services: Preparation and Attitudes." *IFLA Journal* 39, no. 1: 70–78. doi:10.1177/0340035212473089.

———. 2014. "Research Data Management Services in Academic Research Libraries." *Library and Information Science Research* 36, no. 2: 84–90.

Thompson, James. 1982. *The End of Libraries*. London: Clive Bingley.

Wheeler, Carla. 2015. "Ten Takeaways from the 2015 ESRI User Conference. *ArcUser: The Magazine for Esri Software Users* 18, no. 4: 58–59.

Chapter 2

Thinking Differently about Research Library Innovations

THE HISTORICAL LIBRARY INNOVATIONS of the previous chapter demonstrate the factors that can inhibit or facilitate change in the library. Change has always been a factor in organizational life, and organizations change in different ways. However, the rate of change and the resulting success can vary significantly. Innovation is about change, but what kind of change is needed, and what are the factors that bring about change?

Today, organizational leaders are faced with a major challenge in which the continuation of the status quo may result in external events forcing fundamental and even disruptive change in their institutions. Change can disrupt the stability of the organization and can impact social relationships, personal networks, and the delivery of quality service. Local pride in the organization can act in resistance to change and a reluctance to seek new knowledge. A proposed innovation can introduce new vocabulary and unfamiliar jargon, resulting in a "communication differential" and ultimately an obstacle to change (Zaltman, Duncan, and Holbeck 1984, 86–87). Machiavelli ([1532] 1940, 21) best summarizes the dilemma and the resistance to change: "It must be considered that there is nothing more difficult to carry out, nor more doubtful of success, nor more dangerous to handle, than to initiate a new order of things. For the reformer has enemies in all those who profit by the old order."

Library managers and scholars have articulated the necessity to transform the library, although few have been able to articulate a vision of what this transformation should look like. To reinvent the library, two fundamental obstacles will have to be overcome: the uncertainty of all innovation projects and the organizational resistance to change. Uncertainty manifests itself in concerns regarding the ends or outcomes of a new project as well as the means or how the project will be implemented. Resistance to change is always present in social organizations. However, the traditions and norms of the library profession create additional obstacles that can act as barriers to innovation.

Organizational Innovation

Innovation can be studied from three different perspectives. Economists study innovation at the national or cross-national levels, seeking to understand how factors such as R&D funding and entrepreneurship contribute to innovation and economic growth in a country (Crosby 2000; Wong, Ho, and Autio 2005). Innovation can also be studied at the individual level where it is closely associated with creativity and personal characteristics such as motivation and risk taking (Amabile 1996; Hennessey and Amabile 2010). In the 1970s, scholars began to transfer models and methods, used earlier for studying individual innovation, to the study of innovation in organizations.

This text focuses exclusively on organizational innovation in a unique nonprofit institution—the university research library. Although many of us have an intuitive understanding of what constitutes an organization, a definition is always useful as a starting point. Organizations are the major mechanisms for achieving society's goals (Hage and Aiken 1970, 5). Rogers (2003, 404) provides a more formal definition: "An organization is a stable system of individuals who work together to achieve common goals through a hierarchy of ranks and a division of labor."

Organizational innovation represents a specific type of change and occurs in a complex social setting, taking many different forms. Forces in the external environment such as competition and technological advances can stimulate innovation in an organization. In contrast to the relatively stable period of the 20th century, our society today is seemingly more complex, with challenges emanating from many different environmental dimensions—social, economic, political, and technological. Why is the environment important in innovation studies? Burns and Stalker (1961, 105) posed the original insight, indicating that a stable environment produces mechanistic organizations—hierarchical and relatively inflexible. However, a changing and unstable environment will produce an organic structure—flattened and flexible, with many different job types. The rationale for this effect is that leaders in the unstable environment must find ways to cope with the more dynamic environment, resulting in the development of new organizational knowledge and relying less on established rules and processes.

The structure of the organization—size, number of units, hierarchy, and the focus on rules and process—can affect the innovativeness of the organization. Although there are obvious factors such as the strategy of the organization that affect innovation, researchers have also uncovered more subtle influences, such as the effects of an urban or suburban environment (Damanpour and Schneider 2006; Kimberly and Evanisko 1981). Studies have shown how the embedded culture of the organization acts to resist change and preserve the status quo. And, of course, there are the leaders of the organization who establish their imprint on the organization by preserving the culture or, alternatively, by launching out in new directions that result in major change.

What do innovations look like in the nonprofit organization and the research library? There are the more modest incremental innovations that provide enhancements to existing services. These innovations are more routine and typically do not require changes in the structure, processes, or policies of the organization. Examples of incremental innovations in the research library include delivery of bibliographic instruction using online tutorials or the introduction of a device for students to check out books. These innovations require minimal change in organizational structure, practices, and related processes. And then there are the innovations that result in major changes to the organization and what scholars call the radical innovation, one that is always to some extent disruptive of the status quo.[4] Radical innovations involve new knowledge that is used to create totally new products and services or to make fundamental changes in an existing product or service.

---

[4] Although somewhat pejorative, the term *radical* is used in the research literature to designate an innovation that requires new knowledge and is typically accompanied by major changes in the organization.

The Library and the University

The specific organization to be examined in this study is a unique institutional nonprofit—the university research library. A fundamental premise in the text presented here is that a more innovative library is better able to adapt and contribute to scholarship and the advancement of knowledge in the research university. Why study innovation in research libraries? This question cannot be answered without first considering research and the university. Up to 50 percent of all US economic growth over the past 50 years is thought to be the result of investments in research and development (Sonka and Chicoine 2004). Universities in the United States are considered by many to be preeminent because they produce a very high proportion of this research and the associated fundamental knowledge (Cole 2009, 5). At a time of increased scrutiny of higher education, a recent report on the path forward (CGS and ETS 2010, 2) illustrates how the US graduate education system benefits the United States and the world. US graduate schools have had far-reaching accomplishments in the sciences, business, government, education, and the arts, positively affecting millions of people. From 1997 to 2009, over half of the Nobel Prize winners in chemistry, physics, medicine, and economics had received their graduate degrees in the United States. At an increasing pace, American universities awarded 52,760 doctorates in 2013, up 3.5 percent from 2012 and 8 percent over 2011 (Lederman 2014). The report on the path forward illustrates the value of graduate education to both the US economy and our quality of life. Of the approximately 600 universities that offer advanced degrees, only about 125 contribute significantly to the growth of knowledge (Cole 2009, 6). It is the research libraries that are associated with these primary research institutions that are the subject of the analysis in this text.

The research library inherits many of the challenges faced by the research university. James Duderstadt (2000, 3), a former president of the University of Michigan, writes eloquently of these challenges indicating that "obsolescence lies in store for those who cannot, in some manner, adapt to our new reality." Some 30 years ago, Patricia Battin characterized the situation facing the library and the university. Communication technologies have eroded the traditional bonds between librarians and scholars. The university, as one of the most conservative institutions in our society, finds it difficult to view the future in terms of a vastly different organizational structure (Battin 1984). Bass (1985, 160) illustrates the magnitude of this challenge in the university: "Changes are particularly difficult to effect in the public university, embedded as it is in a state of bureaucracy, often further enmeshed in union rules and contracts, as well as departmental and faculty norms and traditions."

The Research Library

In perhaps the simpler environment of the late 19th and early 20th centuries, library visionaries such as Charles Cutter and John Cotton Dana projected an optimistic view of the library, suggesting radical innovations such as collecting non-book materials and the installation of book lifts and "various little railroads" to retrieve books (Musmann 1993, 197–99). These early practitioners envisioned growth and opportunities for the library. However, in today's more dynamic environment, conflicting perceptions have emerged.

Research libraries exist within and derive their mission from the university and must strive to continually evolve with their institutions. This evolution is made more difficult in the multiple subcultures of the university—provosts, administrators, faculty, students, and librarians. These groups hold different perspectives and may, at times, be at odds with each other. Success for these various stakeholders can take on quite different criteria and lead to confusing priorities for the library. Munn (1968) offers an interesting historical perspective, indicating that most universities allocate a relatively small, but remarkably consistent, percent of operating budget to the library. In Munn's day, the allocation was around 4 or 5%. In today's library, this percentage is even smaller and no longer consistent, averaging less than 2% for many research libraries and continuing in a downward trend. Whether this allocation is 10, 5, or 1 percent, it should be based on the impact and value of library services to the university.

The perspective of provosts in guiding the mission of the library is important. However, recent research suggests that these senior administrators have quite varied opinions of what constitutes success and how to judge library impact. Robertson's review (2015) cites various studies indicating that provosts and senior administrators were generally supportive of the library but also had a limited understanding of the library's role in the university. Robertson reports that provosts did not see any evidence of "an existential challenge" to the university library. However, there was ambivalence in the understanding of library skills and the emergence of new roles. Daniel Greenstein (Kolowich 2009), vice provost for academic planning and programs in the University of California system, reflected this ambivalence in offering a somewhat negative view of the possibilities for the library: "The university library of the future will be sparsely staffed, highly decentralized, and have a physical plant consisting of little more than special collections and study areas." His perspective suggests that the research library may be in a downward spiral that will culminate in irrelevance for the university.

For most of modern library history, librarians, researchers, and scholars have articulated the need for change (Alire and Evans 2010; Budd 2001, 328; Conner 2014, 51–57; Martell 2000; Neal 2006; Shera 1966, 95; Smith 1990, 57; Stoffle, Renaud, and Veldof 1996; Stoffle et al. 2003; Taylor 1973, 452; White 1990). These authors have discussed library culture, predicted the future, advocated for more R&D, and posed questions that we need to ask ourselves. They have speculated about the importance of bibliographic control and the role of the information intermediary and suggested that perhaps the library is no longer in the book business. In advocating for a transformation, Stoffle and colleagues (2003, 363) have posited that the "choice is to change and thrive or live in the past and fail." So it is not useful to again state that the research library and librarians must change. There is, however, overwhelming evidence that the rate of change in the external environment, particularly in the advance of technology, is impacting more on the research library than ever before. In this turbulent environment, the research library with a broad knowledge base and an innovative culture will be much better able to contend with rapid and unexpected change.

Traditionally, change and improvement in the library has progressed incrementally—a sequential and, frequently, a painstakingly slow process. From recent interviews with library leaders and scholars within the profession, there is an ongoing dialog about the need to transform the academic library (Alire and Evans 2010, 329–52; Jantz 2012). One of the issues mentioned most frequently by library leaders is the need to address change—not incremental change but "rather dramatic or radical change" (Alire and Evans 2010, 330). In proposing an R&D agenda for academic libraries, James Neal (2006, 3) states, "there will need to be a heightened attention to innovation."

Radical Innovations—Thinking Differently

Introducing more radical innovations will become an important strategy of the research library in order to meet the needs of the 21st-century information society. Risk, uncertainty, faculty norms, miscommunication, university policies, and the creation of new roles in the library remain as persistent obstacles. The opportunity, however, for more innovative initiatives has never been greater. Radical innovations will require library leaders to think quite differently about new services, going beyond continuous improvement to embrace entirely new service concepts.

The process begins with dramatically different concepts that provide new capabilities to faculty and students while also improving efficiency and management practices for the library. Research data management, centers for GIS and digital humanities, and scholarly library publishing all represent opportunities for the creation of new service concepts. Although these new services might be constructed incrementally, innovation must be more at the concept level, demonstrating total value to stakeholders and supporting the strategic transformation of the library. This approach is illustrated in table 2.1, contrasting the continuous improvement of traditional reference service with a new service concept—scholarly library publishing.

TABLE 2.1 The Service Concept and Radical Innovation		
	Continuous Incremental Improvement	**Radical Innovation (a New Service)**
The Service Concept	Reference Service	Scholarly Library Publishing
Service Components	• E-mail reference • Chat reference • Reference outposts • Etc.	• E-journals • E-textbooks • ETDs • Etc.

Although research libraries have created various publishing services, this example demonstrates how one might think more holistically about new services that integrate multiple components using commonly available platforms. Strategic thinking takes into account the benefit for different market segments (students, faculty, university administration) that can be served by library publishing while also reducing overall management overhead and development costs for the library and the university.

A Service Concept—Scholarly Library Publishing

Publishing in its various forms seems to be a natural extension of the traditional library book and journal information services. In an ARL study, Karla Hahn (2007) reported that 44 percent of 80 responding libraries indicated that they were delivering some type of publishing service. In the study of ARL libraries reported here, library leaders were asked if they had made a decision to publish e-journals and to indicate if the service had been fully implemented.[5] Of the 50 responding libraries in 2012, 24 percent indicated that they had fully implemented a journal publishing service. From these survey results, library publishing appears to be making significant inroads as a new service within the university. In order to continue this publishing momentum, the Library Publishing Coalition (LPC) was established in 2012 to advocate for the creation of library publishing services and articulate value for faculty, students, staff, and university stakeholders (LPC 2013). The LPC proposes that libraries build on core values and skills to provide the creation, dissemination, and curation of scholarly works in all digital formats. This advocacy serves an important role for the academic library community in stimulating thinking about the dissemination of knowledge and providing a forum for discussion.

To illustrate a more encompassing service concept, we speculate here on what library publishing might entail. In this approach, a variety of publishing services are brought together in a single unit to offer new capabilities for university clients while also taking advantage of a larger ecosystem of open-source platforms that improve management efficiency and control.

- *Open-access journals.* Publishing open-access journals is built on the premise that scholars will benefit from a new publishing venue that is committed to open access while also reducing costs for scholarly publishing. This service also supports the university open-access initiative and removes many of the price and permission barriers that exist today in the journal-publishing domain. Increasingly, in addition to faculty, undergraduates and graduates

---

[5] See questions 37 and 38 on the innovation survey (Jantz 2013).

can benefit from having an outlet for their publications. Perhaps the most popular publishing platform is Open Journal Systems (OJS) from the Public Knowledge Project, with over 8,200 journals that have published at least 10 articles in a single year (PKP 2015). Of the 115 libraries surveyed for the 2016 version of the Library Publishing Directory (Lippincott, 2015), 43% use the OJS platform for journal publishing.

- *Self-archiving.* Self-archiving, an emerging faculty service, provides for the deposit of preprints and published articles, thereby increasing access and citations. To implement an open-access policy and the associated faculty deposit service, Mullen and Otto (2015) report that there is little in the research literature that details the practical aspects of the scholarly communication organization that a research library will need. These librarians have aptly characterized the challenge and the specific tasks that must be undertaken by the library, including the development of a trusted repository infrastructure, a web portal for deposit and access, communication with every faculty member in the university, and working with academic departments to establish a self-deposit process that meets scholars' needs. DSpace, Fedora, and EPrints are open-source platforms that have been used to provide the self-deposit service.[6]

- *Open e-textbooks.* These textbooks are typically authored by faculty and are motivated by the desire to lower textbook costs for students. The library challenge is to provide the quality and availability for open e-textbooks that is found in the traditional monograph-publishing model.

- *Electronic theses and dissertations.* Many universities are openly publishing dissertations and also scanning historic dissertations for publication. This service supports scholarly communication and the international commitment to open ETDs, while also providing efficiencies to graduate school administration. OpenETD is an open-source, web-based software application for managing

---

[6] For information on DSpace and Fedora, see http://www.duraspace.org. For information on EPrints, see http://www.eprints.org.

the submission, approval, and distribution of electronic theses and dissertations.[7]

- *University press publications.* An increasing number of university presses are now located organizationally in university libraries (Bonn and Furlough 2015, 6). Significant possibilities exist for collaboration with the university press to produce and manage both open-access and revenue-generating publications (Lewis 2013). In 2013, the AAUP launched a study to provide information that would help university press directors and ARL library directors better understand relationships and the potential for collaboration. In survey responses, 62 percent of all respondents (77 percent of library respondents and 34 percent of press respondents) agreed that publishing should be part of the library's mission (AAUP 2013).

- *Related publishing services* include print-on-demand, copyright consultation, marketing (external relations), and collaboration with university administration and university presses.

Holbrook (2015, 52–53) indicates that library publishers are facing a crisis of legitimation and will need to engage their potential users as co-designers. In this effort, strategic questions regarding these new service concepts will need to be addressed, debated, and resolved within the library leadership team. How is this more encompassing concept to be marketed within the university? Is this more holistic publishing concept sustainable or one that merely satisfies a temporary niche in the scholarly world? How is the new service to be situated within the library? From an organizational structure perspective, the more comprehensive service concept would likely require the creation of a new unit in the library with budget control and a certain amount of autonomy to make decisions about future directions. New skills in areas such as marketing and business management will be required. Finally, and perhaps most importantly, these new concepts enable both administrators and faculty to view the library from a different perspective, one of a suite of comprehensive services rather than a place for study and storage of books and journals.

---

[7] For information on OpenETD, see https://rucore.libraries.rutgers.edu/open/projects/openetd.

Conclusion

There are many forces in the external environment that can stimulate a more innovative culture, while a conservative institution, professional norms, and library organizational structures represent persistent impediments to significant change. The academic community has a long way to go before deeply embedded values of both academics and librarians can be changed to enable new means of scholarly communication. Frequently, these opposing forces appear to be in equilibrium, representing a bleak picture for those who are trying to bring about a transformation.

Innovation can become part of the library culture resulting from a "conscious, purposeful search for innovation opportunities" (Drucker 1991, 9). Once these innovation opportunities are uncovered and new service concepts are identified, the library can turn its attention to making them a reality. Whether it is library publishing, research data services, a GIS service center, or totally new service concepts, the question remains: can library leaders and members think more radically and holistically in order to bring these innovations to fruition? The following chapters will address how, in Machiavelli's words, the library can go about initiating this new order of things.

References

AAUP (Association of American University Presses). 2013. *Press and Library Collaboration Survey.* New York: AAUP. http://www.aaupnet.org/images/stories/data/librarypresscollaboration_report_corrected.pdf.

Alire, Camilla A., and G. Edward Evans. 2010. *Academic Librarianship.* New York: Neal-Schuman.

Amabile, Teresa M. 1996. "Creativity and Innovation in Organizations." Harvard Business School Background Note, 396-239 (January).

Bass, Bernard M. 1985. *Leadership and Performance beyond Expectations.* New York: Free Press.

Battin, Patricia. 1984. "The Library: Center of the Restructured University." *College and Research Libraries* 45, no. 3 (May): 170–76. doi:10.5860/crl_45_03_170.

Bonn, Maria, and Mike Furlough. 2015. "The Roots and Branches of Library Publishing Programs." In *Getting the Word Out: Academic Libraries as Scholarly Publishers,* edited by Maria Bonn and Mike Furlough, 1–13. Chicago: Association of College and Research Libraries.

Budd, John M. 2001. *Knowledge and Knowing in Library and Information Science.* Lanham, MD: Scarecrow Press.

———. 2012. *The Changing Academic Library: Operations, Culture, Environments.* Chicago: Association of College and Research Libraries.

Burns, Tom, and G. M. Stalker. 1961. *The Management of Innovation.* London: Tavistock.

CGS (Council of Graduate Schools) and ETS (Educational Testing Service). 2010. *The Path Forward: The Future of Graduate Education in the United States.* Princeton, NJ: ETS. http://www.fgereport.org/rsc/pdf/CFGE_report.pdf.

Cole, Jonathan R. 2009. *The Great American University: Its Rise to Preeminence, Its Indispensable National Role, Why It Must Be Protected.* New York: Public Affairs.

Conner, Matthew. 2014. *The New University Library: Four Case Studies.* Chicago: American Library Association.

Crosby, Mark. 2000. "Patents, Innovation and Growth." *Economic Record* 76, no. 234 (September): 255–62.

Damanpour, Fariborz, and Marguerite Schneider. 2006. "Phases of the Adoption of Innovations in Organizations: Effects of Environment, Organization and Top Managers." *British Journal of Management* 17, no. 3 (September): 215–236.

Drucker, Peter F. 1991. "The Discipline of Innovation." In *Managing Innovation,* edited by Jane Henry and David Walker, 9–17. London: Sage Publications.

Duderstadt, James J. 2000. *A University for the 21st Century.* Ann Arbor: University of Michigan Press.

Hage, Jerald, and Michael Aiken. 1970. *Social Change in Complex Organizations.* New York: Random House.

Hahn, Karla. 2007. "Research Library Publishing Services: New Options for University Publishing. Association of Research Libraries. http://www.arl.org/storage/documents/publications/research-library-publishing-services-mar08.pdf.

Hennessey, Beth A., and Teresa M. Amabile. 2010. "Creativity." *Annual Review of Psychology* 61: 569–98.

Holbrook, J. Britt. 2015. "We Scholars: How Libraries Could Help Us with Scholarly Publishing, if Only We'd Let Them." In *Getting the Word Out: Academic Libraries as Scholarly Publishers,* edited by Maria Bonn and Mike Furlough, 43–54. Chicago: Association of College and Research Libraries.

Jantz, Ronald C. 2012. "Innovation in Academic Libraries: An Analysis of University Librarians' Perspectives." *Library and Information Science Research* 34, no. 1 (January): 3–12. doi:10.1016/j.lisr.2011.07.008.

———. 2013. "Incremental and Radical Innovations—Survey," May 20, doi:10.7282/T37D2S88.

Kimberly, John R., and Michael J. Evanisko. 1981. "Organizational Innovation: The Influence of Individual, Organizational, and Contextual Factors on Hospital

Adoption of Technological and Administrative Innovations." *Academy of Management Journal* 24, no. 4 (December 1): 689–713.

Kolowich, Steve. 2009. "Libraries of the Future." *Inside Higher Ed*, September 24. http://www.insidehighered.com/news/2009/09/24/libraries .

Lederman, Doug. 2014. "Doctorates Up, Career Prospects Not." *Inside Higher Ed*, December 8. https://www.insidehighered.com/news/2014/12/08/number-phds-awarded-climbs-recipients-job-prospects-dropping.

Lewis, David W. 2013. "From Stacks to the Web: The Transformation of Academic Library Collecting." *College and Research Libraries* 74, no. 2 (March): 159–77. doi: 10.5860/crl-309.

Lippincott, Sarah K. 2015. *Library Publishing Directory 2016*. Atlanta, GA: Library Publishing Coalition.

LPC (Library Publishing Coalition). 2013. "Mission." http://www.librarypublishing. org/about-us/mission.

Machiavelli, Niccolò. (1532) 1940. *The Prince*, translated by Luigi Ricci, revised by E. R. P. Vincent. In *The Prince and the Discourses*. New York: Modern Library. (Original work published ca. 1532).

Martell, Charles. 2000. "The Disembodied Librarian in the Digital Age." *College and Research Libraries* 61, no. 1 (January): 10–28.

Mullen, Laura Bowering, and Jane Johnson Otto. 2015. "The Rutgers Open Access Policy: Implementation Planning for Success." *QQML Journal*. doi:10.7282/ T3B56MMQ.

Munn, Robert F. 1968. "The Bottomless Pit, or the Academic Library as Viewed from the Administration Building." *College & Research Libraries* 29: 51-54.

Musmann, Klaus. 1993. *Technological Innovations in Libraries, 1860–1960: An Anecdotal History*. Westport, CT: Greenwood Press.

Neal, James G. 2006. "The Research and Development Imperative in the Academic Library: Path to the Future." *portal: Libraries and the Academy* 6, no. 1 (January): 1–3.

PKP (Public Knowledge Project). 2015. "OJS Usage." https://pkp.sfu.ca/ojs/ojs-usage.

Robertson, Mark. 2015. "Perceptions of Canadian Provosts on the Institutional Role of Academic Libraries." *College and Research Libraries* 76, no. 4 (May): 490–511. doi:10.5860/crl.76.4.490.

Rogers, Everett M. 2003. *Diffusion of Innovations*, 5th ed. New York: Free Press.

Shera, Jesse Hauk. 1966. *Documentation and the Organization of Knowledge*. Hamden, CT: Archon Books.

Smith, Eldred. 1990. *The Librarian, the Scholar, and the Future of the Research Library*. New York: Greenwood Press.

Sonka, Steven T., and David L. Chicoine. 2004. "Value and University Innovation." *American Journal of Agricultural Economics* 86, no. 5: 1337–44.

Stoffle, Carla J., Barbara Allen, David Morden, and Krisellen Maloney. 2003. "Continuing to Build the Future: Academic Libraries and Their Challenges." *portal: Libraries and the Academy* 3, no. 3 (July): 363–80.

Stoffle, Carla J., Robert Renaud, and Jerilyn R. Veldof. 1996. "Choosing Our Futures." *College and Research Libraries* 57, no. 3 (May): 213–25.

Taylor, Robert S. 1973. "Innovation in Libraries: Effect on Function and Organization." In *Toward a Theory of Librarianship: Papers in Honor of Jesse Hauk Shera*, edited by Conrad H. Rawski, 451–62. Metuchen, NJ: Scarecrow Press.

White, Herbert S. 1990. "Libraries and Librarians in the Next Millennium. *Library Journal* 115, no. 9 (May 15): 54–55.

Wong, Poh Kam, Yuen Ping Ho, and Erkko Autio. 2005. "Entrepreneurship, Innovation and Economic Growth: Evidence from GEM Data." *Small Business Economics* 24, no. 3 (April): 335–50. doi:10.1007/s11187-005-2000-1.

Zaltman, Gerald, Robert Duncan, and Jonny Holbeck. 1984. *Innovations and Organizations*. Malabar, FL: Robert E. Krieger.

Chapter 3

The Spread of the Innovation throughout the Organization

ACCORDING TO ROGERS (2003, 5), diffusion "is the process in which an innovation is communicated through certain channels over time among the members of a social system." The social system in this study is the research library and the university, consisting of many interrelated units and organizational members who are engaged in accomplishing common goals. The diffusion of a specific innovation may take several months, extend for many years, or appear to be suspended in time. Complex innovations may be implemented piecemeal, thereby reducing risk and creating a more manageable implementation. There are many intriguing questions regarding the obstacles to the diffusion process and the rate of diffusion throughout society. Contrary to popular opinion, technical superiority does not always govern the rate of diffusion as seen in the following examples.

Rogers (2003, 9–10) relates an account of the non-diffusion of the Dvorak keyboard for typewriters, even though this keyboard layout appeared to be technically superior to the dominant QWERTY keyboard. The Dvorak keyboard reduces the amount of work for each finger and minimizes hand motion, enabling increased typing rates and reducing finger strain. The QWERTY keyboard was optimized to avoid the jamming of typewriter keys. However, the vested interests of manufacturers, sales outlets, and even typing teachers resulted in the QWERTY keyboard becoming the de facto standard. With obsolescence of the typewriter and much technological evolution, we might yet see the diffusion of the Dvorak keyboard and many other arrangements made possible by today's modern operating systems and virtual keyboards.

In the late 19th century, the anti-vibration properties of the pneumatic or air tire for bicycles were not sufficiently attractive for users to adopt it over the solid rubber tire. Skeptics thought that the air tire would prove slippery on muddy roads and bikers would have difficulty keeping the tires inflated. But bike racers soon realized that the air tire provided significant speed advantages, resulting in the rapid diffusion throughout the racing community and the general public (Bijker 1997, 80–85).

The Dvorak keyboard represents a case of non-diffusion, whereas the air tire demonstrates how a small, narrowly focused group can dramatically influence the rate of diffusion. From these examples, one can see that what at first might appear to be a desirable innovation can encounter many obstacles to full implementation and diffusion throughout a social system.

The Innovation Diffusion Process

In spite of the many factors affecting an innovation, scholars have been able to identify the primary stages of a successful diffusion (Rogers 2003, 420–32; Duncan 1976, 168–70). For each of the three major diffusion stages (figure 3.1), there are multiple sub-stages.

FIGURE 3.1
Stages in Rogers's Diffusion of Innovation Model (Rogers 2003, 421)

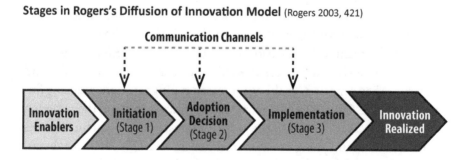

A first step in the initiation stage is organizational awareness of the possibility for an innovation. Leaders might pursue an innovation as a new opportunity or to address an existing problem or performance gap. If leaders have a positive attitude toward change, then initiation of an innovation becomes possible and progresses to the second sub-stage of initiation—attitude formation. This is a critical stage involving the leader, the leadership team, and the strategy of the organization. To move ahead with a decision, the leadership team forms a positive view of the innovation potential, considering issues such as the complexity of the innovation, compatibility with organizational culture and existing services, and potential benefits to the client and the institution.

The subsequent adoption stage focuses on the organizational decision to adopt the innovation and proceed to implementation. Decisions might be made by consensus or, in a more centralized organization, by a relatively few individuals with authority or special expertise. In the adoption stage, there is much information gathering and communication within the leadership team in order to decide to proceed. The decision process will be partially constrained by contextual factors such as the size of the organization, organizational structure, culture, and funding sources.

The implementation stage typically has two sub-stages. In the initial implementation, the innovation is put on a trial basis and evaluated to determine if it is practical for a long-term commitment. The second sub-stage of implementation involves a formal commitment in which the organization establishes appropriate processes and policies and possibly makes structural changes to support the innovation. Full implementation results when a majority of the potential clients have successfully used the innovation. Although figure 3.1 illustrates an orderly and sequential process, in reality there is much feedback, communication, and organizational churn before an innovation is successfully realized. A successful outcome in each of the stages shown in figure 3.1 requires leadership support, considerable flexibility, and persistence in the face of many obstacles.

Innovation Enablers and Ideas

Innovation enablers (figure 3.1) can jump-start the diffusion process and include new knowledge, technological advancements, and competitive threats. Events in the external environment such as new legislation from the state government or a revision of the institution's funding model can precipitate changes in the strategy and structure of the library. Ideas, however, are the antecedents of innovation and the most important enablers.

Ideas originate with individuals and are the starting point for a successful innovation. Darwin's experience on the *Beagle* is instructive. Johnson (2010, 3–7) describes the situation in 1836 on the desolate Keeling Islands in the Indian Ocean. As Darwin wades out into the surf along a live coral reef, he is on "the edge of an idea" and explores a hunch about the paucity of life on land while the reef teems with sea life. We see here a new idea taking shape in the convergence of personal characteristics—curiosity, observation, and motivation. From Darwin's hunch, the theory of evolution ultimately materialized, a concept that has still not thoroughly diffused throughout society.

Ideas are fragile and the path of an idea through the organization is laden with obstacles—a traditional culture, professional norms, local power structures, insufficient resources, inadequate skills, risk, and fear of failure. In the diffusion process, ideas can become disembodied, subject to various external forces, and lost amidst the overriding purpose to serve users. To capture important ideas, the orientation toward innovation must come from the highest levels of management by stimulating an atmosphere of freedom for organizational members to express and test new ideas (Alencar 2012; Amabile 1996; Ekvall 1991).

Classification of Innovations

Innovations proceeding through the diffusion process can be classified according to several different criteria including the type of consumer (end user, administrator, or manager), the magnitude of change, and the perceptions of the innovation itself.

Administrative and Technical Innovations

In a study of public libraries, Damanpour and Childers (1985) emphasize the importance of distinguishing between types of innovations, noting that different effects arise from both organizational factors and the stages of innovation. The most fundamental innovation typology distinguishes between administrative or management innovations and technical innovations. The management innovation focuses on the work and internal processes of the organization and relates to how and what managers do (Damanpour 2014; Hamel 2006). Damanpour and Aravind (2011) summarize this evolving vocabulary noting that administrative or managerial innovations involve new organizational structures, management practices, and processes that improve efficiency whereas technical or service innovations involve new capabilities that are delivered to the end user.

Administrative and technical innovations differ in both characteristics and the process of implementation. Typically, it is management within the administrative core of the organization that is responsible for the introduction of administrative innovations. For example, the HR director might launch an administrative innovation to improve the employee performance review process. These innovations may impact every member of the organization, resulting in a considerable time lapse before the innovation is diffused throughout the organization.

Service innovations are frequently intangible, lacking any physical components, and require integration and close cooperation with the client or end user (Hipp and Grupp 2005).[8] For a university library, technical innovations delivered to the end user usually involve both process and technical components. Although the technical aspects are frequently related to software applications, some innovations include physical devices such as the "self check-out" service that enables students to avoid long lines during peak periods at the circulation desk. This service includes the check-out device and the updated processes for training library staff and providing instructions to students. Almost all library service innovations require close cooperation with the end user, and the associated integration involves simultaneous production and consumption as can be seen in the standard reference desk interaction.

Incremental and Radical Innovations

A most important characteristic deals with the extent of organizational change resulting from an innovation. The magnitude of organizational

---

[8] In this text, to maintain consistency with the bulk of innovation literature, we will continue to designate library service innovations that are delivered to the end user as technical innovations. The important distinction in this text is that technical innovations are delivered to the end user while management innovations relate to the work of the organization and administrative processes.

change and impact varies along a continuum from minor (incremental) to major (radical). According to Zaltman, Duncan, and Holbeck (1984, 24), a radical innovation is always "to some extent disruptive of the status quo" and involves changes in the organization's subsystems, values, incentives, and power structures. Radical innovations involve new knowledge that is used to introduce totally new services or to make fundamental changes in an existing service whereas an incremental innovation is based on existing knowledge to create improvements in a current product or service. Radical innovations represent a clear departure from existing practice whereas incremental innovations are more routine and support current processes and policies (Herrmann, Tomczak, and Befurt 2006).

Innovation Attributes

Another way to classify innovations is by their perceived attributes. According to Rogers (2003, 15), an innovation has five perceived attributes that explain different rates of adoption: (*a*) relative advantage—the degree to which an innovation is perceived as better than the idea it replaces, (*b*) compatibility—the degree to which an innovation is perceived as being consistent with the organization's values and culture, (*c*) complexity—the degree to which an innovation is perceived as difficult to understand and use, (*d*) trialability—the degree to which an innovation lends itself to experimenting and prototyping, and (*e*) observability—the degree to which the results of an innovation are visible to others. In a meta-analysis that examined perceived attributes, Tornatsky and Klein (1982) found that relative advantage and compatibility were positively associated with innovation whereas complexity was negatively related to innovation. These findings are quite intuitive in that a relative advantage and compatibility with the organization are perceptions that will likely cause a leader to proceed with an innovation. However, a more complex innovation may be costly and incur considerable risk with the possibility of failure.

To bring clarity to these different dimensions, the five perceived attributes of an innovation are related to examples of radical and incremental innovations in both the technical and administrative domains of the library. Four research library innovations are highlighted in table 3.1 and include the following: (*a*) membership in a new professional group—for example, a library interested in publishing might join the Library Publishing Coalition; (*b*) library outposts to enhance reference service; (*c*) creation of an R&D unit to do more exploratory work; and (*d*) the development of an institutional repository (IR). The varying perceptions of each innovation demonstrate the challenge in making adoption decisions and proceeding with implementation.

As can be seen in table 3.1, the incremental innovations are compatible with library culture and have low complexity, resulting in a straightforward and low-risk implementation. Making decisions to proceed with radical innovations will be the most difficult. For example, creating an R&D unit not only raises questions about the benefits to the organization but also changes the organizational structure of the library and alters how funding is allocated. Further, as illustrated in table 3.1, there is no effective way to trial the new R&D unit and observe its efficacy.

TABLE 3.1
Innovation Characteristics and Perceived Attributes

	Administrative	Technical or Service
Incremental	*Membership in a new group* • Low relative advantage • High compatibility • Low complexity • Low observability • Low trialability	*Library outposts for reference service* • Low relative advantage • High compatibility • Low complexity • Medium observability • Low trialability
Radical	*Creation of an R&D unit* • High relative advantage • Low compatibility • Moderate complexity • Low observability • Low trialability	*An institutional repository* • High relative advantage • Low compatibility • High complexity • Medium observability • High trialability

Organizational Typology

The innovation process differs significantly across three general sectors: manufacturing, services, and nonprofits. Western, democratic societies are especially proud of their creative culture and the ability to innovate, resulting in a unique environment that generates innovations in unprecedented numbers. However, most of these innovations emerge from for-profit firms, either in those organizations with large R&D investments or from smaller, flexible, and entrepreneurial start-up companies. By and large, this innovative culture is driven by the profit motive and the desire to establish a competitive edge. For nonprofits such as the research library, the primary goal is to advance the public good. Kaplan (2003, 1) cites another compelling reason for the importance of nonprofit innovation. Innovations in the for-profit sector will generally favor commercial interests and the profit motive whereas the nonprofit innovation is likely to be motivated by altruism and concern for the community to be served. If the ability to innovate remains solely in the commercial sector, society will likely never benefit from these more ethically oriented nonprofit innovations.

A rich and varied tradition of innovation studies clearly reveals that the for-profit and nonprofit sectors differ in terms of knowledge base, the actors involved, the relevant institutions, and the innovation process (Malerba 2005, 381). The various sectors or types of organizations are illustrated in figure 3.2. The manufacturing organization produces physical products in which the innovation can be prototyped, viewed, and tested. The service sector includes the most concentrated, knowledge-intensive, and information-intensive services in the modern industrial economy

FIGURE 3.2
Organizational Typology

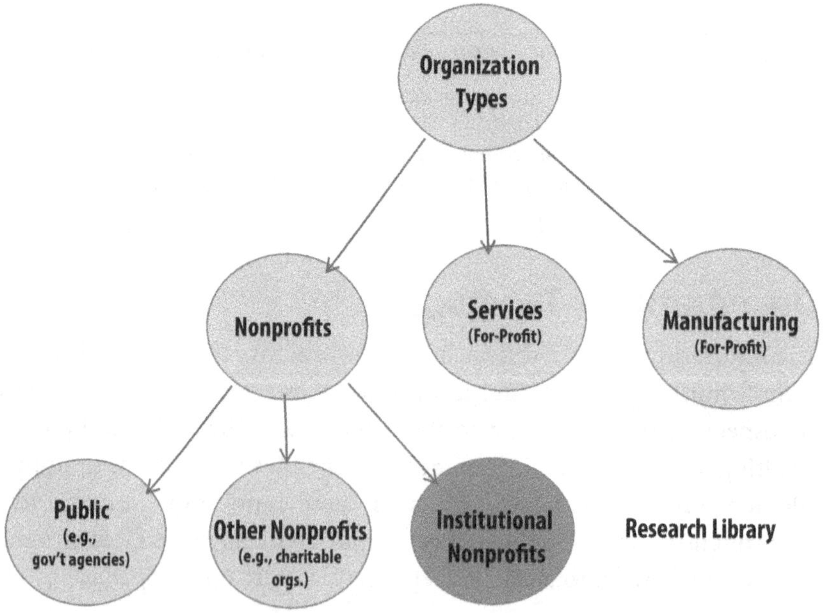

(Miles 2005, 436). There is obviously huge diversity in the service model, ranging from personal services (e.g., hairdressing) to very large firms in areas such as telecommunications, banking, and real estate. The class of nonprofit organizations is quite diverse, including government agencies, community charitable organizations, nonprofit hospitals, and the institutional nonprofit. The characteristics of the organizations in figure 3.2 drive them to innovate in different ways. As indicated in figure 3.2, the university research library is a member of the class of institutional nonprofits—organizations that have well-established professional norms and long-standing traditions.

The Nonprofit Innovation Process

The great body of innovation literature focuses on the for-profit firm, seeking ways for these organizations to improve profits and gain a competitive edge. More recently, innovation scholars (Damanpour, Walker, and Avellaneda 2009; Jaskyte 2011; Walker 2008) have recognized the importance of innovation in nonprofits and how these unique entities advance the public good and contribute to societal goals. The nonprofit service organization must innovate in order to thrive in a rapidly changing world.

The research focus in this text is on those nonprofit organizations that have an institutional and professional framework. The institutional framework is one that is more formal and binding with regulations and well-established traditions. This class of nonprofits includes education (universities, colleges, university libraries, and high schools), teaching hospitals, and certain social services organizations.

Although considerable research has been emerging regarding how the nonprofit innovates, this area of innovation is relatively understudied. Two classic in-depth studies of nonprofits have been published in monograph form. Daft and Becker's (1978) empirical study of innovation in high schools is one of the first that has concentrated on the institutional nonprofit. Among the noteworthy findings was how the leaders' positive attitude toward innovation and decentralized decision making can positively impact innovation. Paul Light (1998) conducted a case study of 26 public organizations including community help groups and government agencies. His model focused on leadership, organizational structure, the environment, and internal management systems. In one finding, Light reports that looser and less bureaucratic management structures provide an organization with the space to innovate (1998, 96). Beyond these in-depth studies, some considerable scholarship has reported on service innovation processes and the factors that affect innovativeness and performance in public service organizations including libraries (Damanpour and Childers 1985; Damanpour and Evan 1984; Damanpour, Walker, and Avellaneda 2009; Deiss 2004; Fowler 1998; Oguz 2015; Reynolds and Whitlach 1985; Salge and Vera 2009; Walker 2008). The study by Damanpour and Childers (1985) of public libraries was one of the first to examine this type of institution, finding that library size is positively related to innovation. Although several of these cited authors have studied libraries and academic institutions in various contexts, the research literature on innovation in institutional nonprofits still remains relatively sparse in comparison to the for-profit sector.

Barras's (1986) model of the reverse product cycle (RPC) was one of first attempts to describe how the nonprofit innovates. In this model, the product cycle acts in the opposite direction from that of manufacturing organizations (Abernathy and Utterback 1978). Thus, innovation begins with incremental, efficiency-oriented innovations, proceeds to quality innovations, and in the third stage culminates in wholly new, radical innovations.

Barras argues that the RPC is enabled by information and communication technologies that are developed elsewhere and then adopted by service organizations. For example, service firms may transfer an information technology product from a manufacturing firm and initially use this technology to improve the efficiency of their back-office processes. Knowledge gained from these incremental innovations might then be used to improve the quality of services offered to clients. As a final stage in the reverse product cycle, the same technology might be incorporated in a more radical and totally new service offering. One can see this progression in research libraries in the initial computerization of administrative records to a more radical use of information and database technology with the introduction of online catalogs and, much later, the institutional repository.

In addition to developing the model of the reverse product cycle, Barras noted other differences in service organizations, including intangible products, minimal formal R&D, and the close linking of product and process innovations. In the service innovation, the human factor is more prominent where both organizational and non-technological knowledge become important (Hipp and Grupp 2005). These innovations are characterized by close contact with customers where delivery involves simultaneous production and consumption of the service. As a result, researchers have had difficulty in measuring the output and productivity of service firms and detecting any improvement (Gallouj and Weinstein 1997, Gallouj and Savona 2009). One can see this challenge in library reference service where the objective is to help increase the knowledge possessed by the student—an objective not easily measured.

One might conclude that effective leadership in a nonprofit such as the research library is even more difficult than in the for-profit sector. Managers in for-profit firms have the benefit of well-defined performance indicators such as profitability or return-on-investment (ROI) to help guide the enterprise and the decision making process. In the for-profit sector, the firm is accountable to both stockholders and customers (Kaplan 2003, 7). If the product doesn't work or the business is not profitable, complaints will be rapidly forthcoming. For a research library, there are no such credible indicators that can provide timely feedback on how the organization is performing. Other than internal measures of efficiency and output (e.g., circulation, gate counts, or file downloads), libraries rarely track and publish value metrics that would be of interest to the parent institution, state governments, and the general public. As a result, the library must frequently rely on user surveys or anecdotal evidence to determine the effectiveness of a new service.

Ethical norms also distinguish the differences between the nonprofit and for-profit sectors. These norms comprise expectations and constraints that are held within the profession and provide guidelines for decision making (Rubin 1990, 213). For example, libraries emphasize the importance of delivering quality service to *all* users (ALA [1939] 2008). Ethical norms can create dilemmas when making the right decisions on behalf of the library user. Of special note are technology-based innovations that raise questions regarding the value of the innovation— value for whom and how much value accrues from the innovation (Budd 2008, 129–33).

Conclusion

Coproduction captures the essence of almost all library innovations where participation of the client—student, staff, and faculty—is involved, thus increasing the importance of marketing and clarifying benefits to the end user. As Barras suggests, we might expect a radical innovation to build on a long series of incremental innovations, enabling the library to develop new knowledge and competencies and reduce the risk of a major new technology. The complexity of the innovation and compatibility with the existing library culture will continue to be major obstacles to more radical innovations in the research library. The parent institution can inhibit or promote innovation; the bureaucracy and obsession with process and rules can restrict the generation of new ideas; and the norms and traditions of the library profession can raise barriers to innovation. In addition, the library leader does not have the benefit of more quantitative indicators to guide the decision process. Given these perspectives, what would motivate research library leaders to undertake the implementation of a radical innovation, possibly incurring considerable risk? In the following chapters, the theory and empirical results from a study of 50 ARL libraries provide significant insight into this dilemma.

References

Abernathy, W. J., and James Utterback. 1978. "Patterns of Innovation in Technology." *Technology Review* 80, no. 7 (June–July): 40–47.

ALA (American Library Association). (1939) 2008. *Code of Ethics of the American Library Association.* http://www.ala.org/advocacy/proethics/codeofethics/codeethics.

Alencar, Eunice M. L. Soriana de. 2012. "Creativity in Organizations: Facilitators and Inhibitors." In *Handbook of Organizational Creativity*, edited by Michael D. Mumford, 87–111. Waltham, MA: Academic Press.

Amabile, Teresa M. 1996. "Creativity and Innovation in Organizations." Harvard Business School Background Note, 396-239 (January).

Barras, Richard. 1986. "Toward a Theory of Innovation in Services." *Research Policy* 15, no. 4 (August): 161–73.

Bijker, Wiebe E. 1997. *Of Bicycles, Bakelites, and Bulbs: Toward a Theory of Sociotechnical Change.* Cambridge, MA: MIT Press.

Budd, John M. 2008. *Self-Examination: The Present and Future of Librarianship.* Westport, CT: Libraries Unlimited.

Daft, Richard L., and Selwyn W. Becker. 1978. *Innovation in Organizations: Innovation Adoption in School Organizations.* New York: Elsevier.

Damanpour, Fariborz. 2014. "Footnotes to Research on Management Innovation." *Organization Studies* 35, no. 9 (September): 1265–85. doi: 10.1177/0170840614539312.

Damanpour, Fariborz, and Deepa Aravind. 2011. "Managerial Innovation: Conceptions, Processes, and Antecedents." *Management and Organization Review* 8, no. 2 (July): 423–54.

Damanpour, Fariborz, and Thomas Childers. 1985. "The Adoption of Innovation in Public Libraries." *Library and Information Science Research* 7, no. 3: 231–46.

Damanpour, Fariborz, and William M. Evan. 1984. "Organizational Innovation and Performance: The Problem of 'Organizational Lag.'" *Administrative Science Quarterly* 29, no. 3 (September): 392–409.

Damanpour, Fariborz, Richard M. Walker, and Claudia N. Avellaneda. 2009. "Combinative Effects of Innovation Types and Organizational Performance: A Longitudinal Study of Service Organizations." *Journal of Management Studies* 46, no. 4 (June): 650–75.

Deiss, Kathryn. 2004. "Innovation and Strategy: Risk and Choice in Shaping User-Centered Libraries." *Library Trends* 53, no. 1: 17–32. http://hdl.handle.net/2142/1717.

Duncan, R. B. 1976. "The Ambidextrous Organization: Designing Dual Structures for Innovation." In *The Management of Organization Design: Strategies and Implementation,* edited by Ralph H. Killman, Louis R. Pondy, and Dennis P. Slevin, 167–88. New York: North-Holland.

Ekvall, G. 1991. "The Organizational Culture of Idea-Management: A Creative Climate for the Management of Ideas." In *Managing Innovation,* edited by Jane Henry and David Walker, 73–79. London: Sage Publications.

Fowler, Rena K. 1998. "The University Library as Learning Organization for Innovation: An Exploratory Study." *College and Research Libraries* 59, no. 3 (May): 220–31.

Gallouj, Faïz, and Maria Savona. 2009. "Innovation in Services: A Review of the Debate and a Research Agenda." *Journal of Evolutionary Economics* 19, no. 2: 149–72.

Gallouj, Faïz, and Olivier Weinstein. 1997. "Innovation in Services." *Research Policy* 26, no. 4/5: 537–56.

Hamel, Gary. 2006. "The Why, What and How of Management Innovation." *Harvard Business Review* 84, no. 2 (February): 72–84.

Herrmann, Andreas, Torsten Tomczak, and Rene Befurt. 2006. "Determinants of Radical Product Innovations." *European Journal of Innovation Management* 9, no. 1: 20–43.

Hipp, Christiane, and Hariolf Grupp. 2005. "Innovation in the Service Sector: The Demand for Service-Specific Innovation Measurement Concepts and Typologies." *Research Policy* 34, no. 4 (May): 517–35.

Jaskyte, Kristina. 2011. "Predictors of Administrative and Technological Innovations in Nonprofit Organizations." *Public Administration Review* 71, no. 1 (January/February): 77–86. doi:10.1111/j..2010.02308.x.

Johnson, Steven. 2010. *Where Good Ideas Come From.* New York: Riverside Books.

Kaplan, Howard B. 2003. *Organizational Innovation: Studies of Program Change in Community Agencies.* New York: Kluwer Academic/Plenum Publishers.

Light, Paul C. 1998. *Sustaining Innovation: Creating Nonprofit and Government Organizations That Innovate Naturally.* San Francisco: Jossey-Bass.

Malerba, Franco. 2005. "Sectoral Systems: How and Why Innovation Differs across Sectors." In *The Oxford Handbook of Innovation,* edited by Jan Fagerberg, David C. Mowery, and Richard R. Nelson, 380–406. Oxford: Oxford University Press.

Miles, Ian. 2005. "Innovation in Services." In *The Oxford Handbook of Innovation,* edited by Jan Fagerberg, David C. Mowery, and Richard R. Nelson, 433–58. Oxford: Oxford University Press.

Oguz, Fatih. 2015. "Organizational Influences in Technology Adoption Decisions: A Case Study of Digital Libraries." *College and Research Libraries,* preprint (accepted May 2015; anticipated publication May 2016). http://crl.acrl.org/content/early/2015/06/11/crl15-695.full.pdf+html.

Reynolds, Judy, and Jo Bell Whitlatch. 1985. "Academic Library Services: The Literature of Innovation." *College and Research Libraries* 46, no. 5 (September): 402–17.

Rogers, Everett M. 2003. *Diffusion of Innovations,* 5th ed. New York: Free Press.

Rubin, Hank. 1990. "Dimensions of Institutional Ethics: A Framework for Interpreting the Ethical Context of the Nonprofit Sector." In *The Nonprofit Organization: Essential Readings,* edited by David L. Gies, J. Steven Ott, and Jay M. Shafritz, 211–16, Pacific Grove, CA: Brooks/Cole Publishing.

Salge, T. O., and A. Vera. 2009. "Hospital Innovativeness and Organizational Performance: Evidence from English Public Acute Care." *Health Care Management Review* 34, no. 1: 54–67. doi:10.1097/01.HMR.0000342978.84307.80.

Tornatzky, Louis G., and Katherine J. Klein. 1982. "Innovation Characteristics and Innovation Adoption-Implementation: A Meta-analysis of Findings." *IEEE Transactions on Engineering Management* 29, no. 1 (February): 28–43.

Walker, Richard M. 2008. "An Empirical Evaluation of Innovation Types and Organizational and Environmental Characteristics: Towards a Configuration Framework." *Journal of Public Administration Research and Theory* 18, no. 4: 591–615.

Zaltman, Gerald, Robert Duncan, and Jonny Holbeck. 1984. *Innovations and Organizations.* Malabar, FL: Robert E. Krieger.

Part Two
THE EMPIRICAL
ANALYSIS

Chapter 4

The Research Model and Innovation in the Research Library

WHAT WE KNOW ABOUT organizations resides in multiple disciplines—organizational behavior, leadership studies, organizational performance, the management of innovation, and the broader area of innovation studies. The resulting theories from these disciplines have been used here to create a research model that encompasses much of the context of the research library and provides a conceptual structure that can be used to accept or reject hypotheses about a specific phenomenon. The model described herein rests on the assumption that organizations, and specifically research libraries, with similar technologies and environmental challenges will behave in similar ways. The approach to uncovering these behavioral patterns is based on theory and the accumulation of data that describes various aspects of the research library. To capture this larger context of the library, data was obtained from both publicly available resources and the perceptions of the library leadership teams. If the model and supporting theory are sound and the data reliable, we should come away with a better understanding of how the research library innovates.

In the preliminary analysis, we examined and speculated on the contribution to innovation of many different factors in the research library environment, resulting in many interesting and unanswered questions. What are the effects of organizational structure on innovation? Does the ratio of support staff to professional staff affect innovation? How does a declining budget over many years affect innovativeness? What are the effects of a large, dynamic metropolitan environment as compared to the more sedate suburban and rural environments? How do the educational backgrounds of the leadership team impact innovation? How is exploratory work funded?

Following on this preliminary analysis, the research model was formulated to take into account the impact of a dynamic external environment and organizational complexity on the innovativeness of the library. Innovativeness in research libraries was hypothesized to be the consequence of five major factors: the actions of the leadership team, the external environment, the organizational structure, the flexibility of the organization, and the size of the library. In addition to these major factors, the demographics of the leadership team and other possible enablers were included in this study because of support in the established literature or because these variables might have causal effects within the unique environment of the research library. The model and hypotheses for exploring the effects of these factors on the innovativeness of the research library are shown in figure 4.1.

In this model, the leadership team, organizational structure, and the external environment are shown to have a direct impact on the innovativeness of the research library. In addition, the leadership team acts through

FIGURE 4.1
The Research Model for Innovativeness in Research Libraries

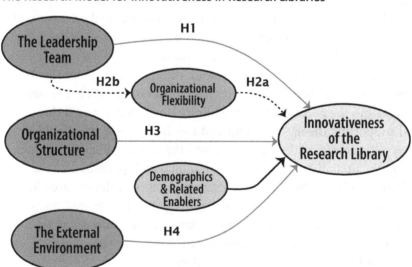

a factor, here called organizational flexibility, to also affect innovativeness. The demographics of the leadership team—age, tenure, education—and related enablers were also examined as having a possible effect on the ability to innovate. As we discuss the related hypotheses, each factor will be defined in more detail, leading to the regression model and the empirical results for the 50 ARL libraries in the study sample.

Hypotheses Relating to the Innovativeness of the Research Library

The Leadership Team

A primary thesis of this study is that the senior leadership of the research library—the top management team (TMT)[9] — has a major impact on innovation. Few researchers will disagree that the leadership team in an organization can have a profound effect on innovation and performance. As Tushman and colleagues (2002) have indicated, the strategy emanating from senior leadership and the resulting organizational design are powerful levers that enable an organization to pursue dramatically different types of activities. To successfully innovate, TMT collaboration and active engagement are needed to create the strategies and supportive structures for an innovative organizational culture. Hambrick (1994, 175) has summarized some of the distinctive attributes of the top management group, noting that these leaders have extremely complex tasks in setting the mission, developing strategy, and dealing with major decisions while also engaging in day-to-day administrative actions.

Building on upper echelons theory,[10] Hambrick (1994, 1995) proposed the concept of *behavioral integration* in the top management team and linked the concept to organizational outcomes. The leadership of an organization is called upon to make decisions in a complex environment

---

[9] The phrase *top management team* has been adopted by organization theorists to refer to the relatively small group of the most influential executives at the apex of the organization (Hambrick 1994, 173). In university libraries, this group typically consists of the university librarian, associate university librarians, and directors.

[10] Upper echelons theory states that organizational culture is a reflection of the top managers' personality traits and demographics (Carpenter, Geletkanycz, and Sanders 2004).

of information overload that is often ambiguous and contradictory and frequently subject to multiple interpretations. According to Hambrick, an integrated team can navigate the complexities of decision making more effectively. However, for many organizations, the concept of a leadership "team" is a misnomer. The group that is nominally the TMT may have little interaction and rarely meets as a team, and group members may have their own agendas. Even in this less integrated team, the leaders and managers of the organization, with their respective styles, competencies, motives, biases, and experience, can be expected to significantly affect organizational outcomes.

Behavioral integration should not be confused with social integration or interdependence. This construct also does not imply consensus and, in fact, behaviorally integrated teams may have considerable disagreement—a situation that can create more content-rich discussions (Hambrick 1994). Hambrick theorized that behavioral integration consists of three important factors: (a) level of collaborative behavior, (b) quantity and quality of information exchange, and (c) emphasis on joint decision making. Scholars have used these leadership characteristics and the behavioral integration construct to study innovation in a variety of settings. Hambrick hypothesizes that a more behaviorally integrated TMT will be better able to deal with the inherent conflicts that emerge in the various stages of the innovation diffusion process.

The position in this study is that behavioral integration of the library TMT is especially important for research libraries to become more innovative. These libraries have focused primarily on incremental innovations that improve efficiency and quality whereas radical innovations that deviate from the norms and traditions of the profession are relatively rare. The radical innovation enables major new services with new users within both student and faculty ranks, but these innovations can be difficult to implement, displacing current services and causing a restructuring of the library.

A behaviorally integrated team has the confidence and trust to have open debates on unpopular issues and risky proposals, resulting in a greater likelihood of achieving agreement and concerted action on controversial projects. The collaborative aspect of the behavioral construct suggests that team members will be more willing to discuss unique, nontraditional ideas. Siegel and Hambrick (1996) have shown that the more behaviorally integrated team makes better use of knowledge alternatives. Through increased quality and quantity of information, more ideas are available for discussion and joint agreement. The flow of new ideas, the willingness to discuss controversial concepts, and the collaborative aspects of the team will lead to more radical innovation proposals flowing into the decision process. In contrast, members of the less behaviorally integrated team are likely to withdraw into their own domains where they have undisputed control. In this behavior, which is typical of the classical manager, rules and processes become dominant and lead to support of the status quo and, at best, more incremental innovations.

The primary way that the TMT influences organizational outcomes results from their role in developing and articulating organizational strategy and creating the resultant organizational structures, policies, and processes. However, perhaps unique to organizations that are embedded in an institutional environment, the TMT not only has a role in overcoming institutional resistance but must also help guide the prospective innovation through the bureaucratic structures that have resulted from many years of professional development and long-held traditions. The collaborative aspect of the behaviorally integrated team becomes important in facilitating the implementation of innovative projects through the various units of the organization. The engagement of the senior team[11] in facilitating innovation projects also provides psychological protection for organizational members who might otherwise be reluctant to work on controversial projects (Un 2010). These team characteristics can result in a strategic mix of both incremental and radical innovations, leading to the following hypothesis:

> **H1:** The extent of behavioral integration of the leadership team is positively associated with innovation performance in the research library. More integration of the senior team will lead to improved innovation performance.

---

[11] The phrases *leadership team, top management team,* and *senior team* are used interchangeably in this text.

Organizational Flexibility—The Ambidextrous Orientation

Achieving long-term success will require the library to meet the demands of current users while also developing new services for the future. The organization will need to be flexible in developing new knowledge while also exploiting existing knowledge to further enhance current services. Organizational scholars refer to this flexibility as an *ambidextrous orientation*.

The concept of ambidexterity originates in the capability of a person to use both hands with equal ease and has become a useful metaphor in organization research. In the research literature, scholars (Duncan 1976; O'Reilly and Tushman 2004; O'Reilly and Tushman 2008; Tushman and O'Reilly 1996) have identified the ability to manage both evolutionary and revolutionary change as an ambidextrous orientation, enabling the organization to become more creative and adaptable. Ambidexterity not only requires the organization to achieve a balance between exploratory and exploitative actions, but also to sustain the balance over time in order to become a truly innovative organization. A key question relates to balance: that is, the ability to do both exploratory and exploitative work but not to put undue emphasis on either activity. According to March (1991), finding a balance is particularly difficult because of the inherent organizational conflicts that emerge from exploration and exploitation. The simple idea underlying ambidexterity is that the demands of an organization's task environment are always, to some extent, in conflict (Gibson and Birkinshaw 2004).

If leaders pursue an ambidextrous orientation, the organization may take on a variety of characteristics that will result in ambidexterity. There are multiple paths that lead to an ambidextrous organization.[12] In a spatial approach similar to the classic R&D organization, firms use two structures simultaneously as an ambidextrous approach to achieve balance (Grover, Purvis, and Segars 2007). For example, innovative activities may be pursued within a single exploratory unit that is buffered from the daily activities supporting existing services.

In a contextual approach (Andriopoulos and Lewis 2009), behavioral and social means are used to manage the varied tasks of exploration and exploitation. For example, leaders may pursue an organization-wide

---

[12] The phrase *ambidextrous orientation* and the term *ambidexterity* will be used interchangeably in this study.

policy that encourages all members to use their own judgment to divide their time between diverse activities that will lead to different types of innovations. In this ambidextrous organization, these diverse activities are valued and rewarded, and failures are recognized as opportunities for learning.

From a temporal perspective, an organization may have long periods of relatively stable incremental improvement occasionally punctuated by the development of a major new capability (Andriopoulos and Lewis 2009; Gersick 1991; Hannan and Freeman 1984; Piao 2010). O'Reilly and Tushman (2008) suggest that leaders do not need to make these temporal tradeoffs by focusing on either exploitation or exploration. Rather, these researchers view ambidexterity as a capability embedded in senior leadership's learning that enables them to reconfigure the organization to adapt to specific circumstances, thus simultaneously supporting both exploratory and exploitative activities.

In the ARL study, we viewed organizational ambidexterity as a strategy for simultaneously improving existing services while exploring and developing major new capabilities. The study explores the senior team's strategy and perspectives regarding the organization's ability to seek greater efficiency and improvements in existing services while also experimenting and developing new knowledge and new services. The measure of an ambidextrous orientation is based on the approach used by Lubatkin and colleagues (2006), who adapted Benner and Tushman's (2003) conceptualization, capturing both dimensions of exploration and exploitation. It is expected that an ambidextrous orientation will result in more balanced investments in different types of innovations, leading to the following hypothesis:

> **H2a:** An ambidextrous orientation is positively related to the innovation performance of the research library. More ambidexterity will result in improved innovation performance.

The leadership team obviously has an impact on the ambidexterity of the organization. As a result, a more integrated team is in a much better position to deal with the conflicts and tensions that result from an ambidextrous orientation. As illustrated in figure 4.1, it is expected that the leadership team will also impact the flexibility of the organization, resulting in improved innovation performance.[13] This observation leads to the following hypothesis:

> **H2b:** A more integrated senior leadership team will positively affect the ambidexterity of the research library, an effect that in turn will enhance innovation performance.

Organizational Structure

The concept of organizational structure can take on several meanings. For this study, we use the definition of primary structure that includes the formal structure found in an organization chart—hierarchy, supporting units, and job descriptions for organizational members. Structural contingency theory suggests that organizations will change their structure in order to align with strategy and adapt to events in the external environment (Galunic and Eisenhardt 1994, 215–19). For example, a research library might launch a new service based on witnessing the success of similar services in peer institutions. Emerging new technologies in the commercial sector might also motivate the library to explore new services based on these technologies. Independent of these external events, library leaders might initiate structural change to better support more innovative projects or to address a performance gap. In this respect, organizational structure becomes a means to facilitate the generation of new ideas and the successful implementation of these ideas.

Duncan (1976, 167) has identified the persistent dilemma for innovative organizations—"different organizational structures appear to be appropriate for the initiation and implementation stages of the innovation process." In the initiation stage, a looser organization with less formalism and hierarchy will allow for the free flow of ideas that can become innovations. However, in the implementation stage, more emphasis on process is needed to meet the schedule, quality, and reliability requirements of the new product or service. Dess, Lumpkin, and McGee (1999) have argued that firms must embrace a barrier-free organization to facili-

---

[13] Statistically, this effect is known as *mediation*, in which an initial causal variable (behavioral integration of the TMT) can influence the dependent variable (innovation performance) through a mediating variable (ambidextrous orientation).

tate knowledge growth in order to overcome the impediments of hierarchical organizational structures.

In this study, *structural differentiation*—the subdivision of library tasks into different units of the library—is an important factor that is expected to impact innovative capability. Structural differentiation results in spatially dispersed units in which exploratory and production activities are structurally separated. Jansen and colleagues (2009) state that structural differentiation can help organizations simultaneously conduct both exploratory and exploitative activities and deal more effectively with the resulting organizational tension. Damanpour and Gopalakrishnan (1998) supported this perspective by noting that organizations in unstable environments will need specialized units to introduce more radical innovations. Earlier studies (Hage and Aiken 1967; Kimberly and Evanisko 1981) have shown that organizational complexity characterized by the variety and number of different units is positively related to innovation. However, as reported by Daft and Becker (1978, 140), there is considerable research suggesting that similar structures support cross-fertilization and information exchange—activities that can lead to more innovation, whereas different structures act as barriers that impede communication.

The structural conundrum is evident in these research studies. To stimulate knowledge growth, it appears that separate structures are needed that are somewhat buffered from the organizational units that conduct the day-to-day business of the library. However, more and different structures apparently limit communication throughout the organization. What appears to be important is not just the structural differentiation, but also the type of structures that are emerging in the research library and how well these structures are integrated (Nord and Tucker 1987, 14–15). In today's library, it is expected that the classical structures, even with more differentiation, and centralized authority persist and continue to represent barriers to the free flow of ideas across units. These observations lead to the following hypothesis:

> **H3:** A more structurally differentiated research library
> will be negatively related to innovation performance.
> More differentiation will result in reduced innovation
> performance.

The External Environment

Although individuals frequently originate innovations within the organization, scholars suggest that many innovations are stimulated by external events, either threats or opportunities. Although there is considerable literature on innovation and public institutions, Noordegraaf and Stewart (2000) suggest that more attention should be given to the environment in which the institution is embedded. During difficult times, possibly created by technological advances or changing economic circumstances, an organization becomes more vulnerable to the influences from external forces. The members of the organization, including the leaders, will typically continue to follow their daily routines until there is some external event that forces a change. In the innovation literature, these events are referred to as jolts, trigger events, or shocks (Van de Ven 1986). Within the nonprofit sector, these external stimuli are more subtle and less compelling than in the for-profit sector that relies on competitor actions and performance metrics for credible feedback. Lacking this feedback, what factors in the external environment might cause library leaders to introduce major change?

Turbulence in the external environment can cause leaders to take action to address the uncertainty. These actions can result in changing the organizational structure or hiring people with different knowledge and skills, initiatives that can ultimately benefit innovation outcomes. However, as Anderson and Tushman (2001) explain, uncertainty can be quite hazardous for an organization. For example, a library may try to adapt to a major new technological advancement, only to find that this technology is quickly rendered obsolete.

Past research indicates that environmental uncertainty affects all types of innovations. In a meta-analysis of 21 studies, Damanpour (1996) found that structural complexity is more positively related to innovation in organizations that are operating under high environmental uncertainty in contrast to those operating under low uncertainty. Germain (1996) examined logistics innovation that involves the organizational-wide flow of goods and information. University libraries are good candidates for this type of innovation in that they store and process millions of books and thousands of digital files while managing a diverse set of information regarding user accounts and bar-coded materials. Although Germain's study focused on manufacturing organizations, his conclusions are noteworthy, indicating that size and environmental uncertainty were definite predictors of radical innovations. Sidhu, Volberda, and Commandeur (2004) have shown that a more dynamic environment will result in an organization conducting more exploratory activities, an important prerequisite to stimulating innovations.

It is the premise of this study that research libraries are finding themselves in a more unstable and less predictable environment. The crucial aspect of the environment is dynamism or the unpredictability of change (Boyne and Meier 2009). The source of this unpredictability typically emanates from the political environment, budget and financial pressures, and the rapid evolution in the technological infrastructure. As Kanter (1983, 280–81) has indicated, the environment does not really create change automatically or directly; rather, it is the perceptions of the environment and related actions by key actors that result in change. Following on this observation, *environmental uncertainty* is defined as an individual's perceived inability to accurately predict events in the external environment.

Leaders that view the environment as benign and stable are not likely to take the actions necessary to introduce innovations into their organization. In contrast, an environmentally aware leadership team will be more responsive to changing conditions in the external environment and more likely to support innovative initiatives. These observations lead to the following hypothesis:

> **H4:** Uncertainty in the external environment, as perceived by library leaders, is positively related to innovation performance in the research library. The perception of more uncertainty will lead to improved innovation performance.

The Regression Model

With these hypotheses, the regression model takes the more specific form, as shown in figure 4.2, in which the independent variables are represented and where plus and minus signs indicate the hypothesized impact on the innovation performance of the library. In the regression analysis, we controlled for both organizational size and the type of institution (public or private) in order to eliminate the unique effects of these variables.

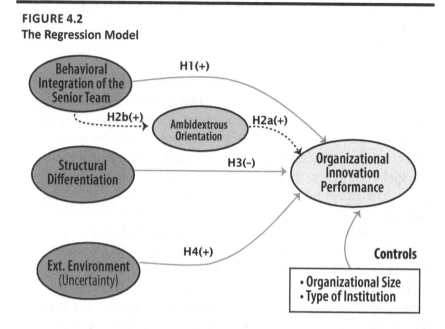

FIGURE 4.2
The Regression Model

Methodology

The phrase *empirical analysis* has been used previously in this text and is an important aspect of the methodology in this study. Empirical analysis goes beyond observation and description and involves making predictions based on data from first-hand observations (Simon 2003, 5–9). In this study, the observations were obtained from the leadership team of each ARL library. The specific type of analysis used here is referred to as hierarchical or sequential regression. In this approach, the researcher enters the independent variables into the analysis based on an order supported by theory (Warner 2013, 559).

Population and Sample

The Association of Research Libraries (ARL) is a nonprofit organization of research libraries at comprehensive, research-intensive institutions in the United States and Canada that share similar research missions, aspirations, and achievements. From the population of US libraries, the author created a sample of 50 libraries by contacting university librarians and obtaining approval for their leadership teams to participate in the innovation study. These library directors typically selected three or four members of the leadership team to participate in the innovation study. The average team size was 3.6 members including the university librarian. Online surveys were sent to the university librarian and the library top management team for the sample of 50 research libraries. Library leaders responded to statements regarding their attitudes toward change, the external environment, ambidexterity, the management team, organizational structure, demographics, and which innovations their institution has adopted. (For the complete survey, see Jantz 2013).

Table 4.1 depicts the size and institutional characteristics of the 50 research libraries in the sample. The size category with the largest number of libraries is the 200–299 FTE range at 32 percent. The research libraries in the sample are predominantly part of public institutions (84.0%) and mostly reside in urban/city environments (84.0%).

TABLE 4.1
Size and Institutional Characteristics of Research Libraries (N = 50)

Size (Total FTE)	Percentage	Number
100–199	30.0	15
200–299	32.0	16
300–399	16.0	8
400–499	10.0	5
≥ 500	12.0	6
Total	100.0	50

Institutional Characteristics	Percentage	Number
Type of Institution (Public/Private)	84.0/16.0	42/8

Geographic Characteristics	Percentage	Number
Region—Urban/City	84.0	42
Region—Suburb	10.0	5
Region—Town	6.0	3
Total	100.0	50

FIGURE 4.3
Geographical Distribution of Research Library Organizations (*N* = 50)

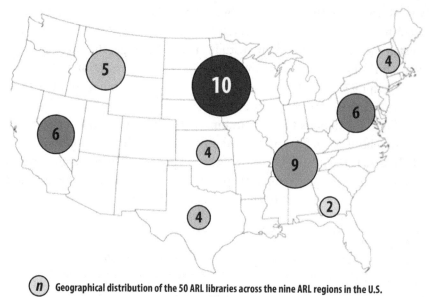

(*n*) Geographical distribution of the 50 ARL libraries across the nine ARL regions in the U.S.

Figure 4.3 illustrates the distribution of the research library organizations across nine geographical regions. For statistical validity, tests of both size and geographical region were conducted to determine if there was any significant difference between the libraries responding to the survey and those not responding. The tests demonstrated that there was no nonresponse bias in either the size of the library or the geographical region. The detailed tests are described in appendix E.

Innovation Performance—The Dependent Variable

A metric constructed from a single dimension is inadequate to represent the complex processes involved in organizational innovation (Ravichandran 2000). In this study, the innovation performance construct—the dependent variable—is defined as consisting of three dimensions that relate to the library's innovative capabilities. These dimensions are aggregated to form the innovation performance construct.

First, the innovation adoption decision reflects the ability of the organization to make a decision to proceed with implementation. To gather the data, survey respondents were asked if they had made a "decision to adopt" for each of 32 library innovations (appendix A). The resulting indicator, sometimes referred to as *innovation magnitude* (Gopalakrishnan 2000), represents the breadth and depth of innovation and is compiled from the organization's decisions regarding the implementation of selected innovations. However, the innovation adoption decision only partially reflects the organization's ability to innovate.

After the decision to adopt is made, the organization must marshal resources to implement the innovation. Walker's configuration framework for service organizations helps us understand why this issue is important for research libraries. Walker (2008) suggests that public organizations may make innovation decisions in search of legitimacy. An innovation decision may be made to manipulate appearances with little effort invested in actually implementing the innovation. Innovation must therefore be more than just an idea or a decision; the innovation must be implemented and have significant user impact. It is possible that a decision is made to adopt an innovation; however, the implementation is never undertaken because of resource constraints, political controversy, or other blocking factors. For the second component of the innovation performance construct, the decision to adopt is augmented by the extent of implementation of the innovation and represents the organization's effort that is directed to realizing the innovation.

The third dimension of innovation performance addresses the flexibility of the library and the ability to simultaneously conduct both exploratory and exploitative activities that can result in both incremental and radical innovations (He and Wong 2004). The traditional culture and bureaucratic structures of the library can resist the implementation of more radical innovations. Research libraries typically create predominantly incremental innovations that emanate from practice and the client interface (Salge and Vera 2009; Sidhu, Volberda, and Commandeur 2004). In a seminal article, March (1991) has stressed the importance of balance that is critical for the firm to survive and prosper. In this study, the innovation performance construct captures the notion of balance and penalizes the library that is implementing either predominantly incremental or predominantly radical innovations.

Independent Variables

From figure 4.2, four independent variables are shown to have impact on the innovativeness of the research library. Two control variables—size of the library and type of institution—were also included in the regression analysis. The more detailed explanation of how these variables were constructed is included in appendix B.

Conclusion

In the research model, a new and more encompassing indicator of innovation performance was created. Hypotheses were proposed as to how various phenomena will impact innovativeness in the research library. A sample of ARL libraries, statistically balanced by size and geographical location, was selected for the regression analysis. In the following chapters, we discuss the findings regarding each hypothesis and report on the unexpected results regarding leadership demographics.

References

Anderson, Philip, and Michael L. Tushman. 2001. "Organizational Environments and Industry Exit: The Effects of Uncertainty, Munificence and Complexity." *Industrial and Corporate Change* 10, no. 3: 675–711.

Andriopoulos, Constantine, and Marianne W. Lewis. 2009. "Exploitation-Exploration Tensions and Organizational Ambidexterity: Managing Paradoxes of Innovation." *Organization Science* 20, no. 4: 696–717.

Benner, Mary J., and Michael L. Tushman. 2003. "Exploration, Exploitation, and Process Management: The Productivity Dilemma Revisited." *Academy of Management Review* 28, no. 2 (April): 238–56.

Boyne, George A., and Kenneth J. Meier. 2009. "Environmental Turbulence, Organizational Stability, and Public Service Performance." *Administration and Society* 40, no. 8 (January): 799–824.

Carpenter, Mason A., Marta A. Geletkanycz, and Wm. Gerard Sanders. 2004. "Upper Echelons Research Revisited: Antecedents, Elements, and Consequences of Top Management Team Composition." *Journal of Management* 30, no. 6 (November): 749–78. doi:10.1016/j.jm.2004.06.001.

Daft, Richard L., and Selwyn W. Becker. 1978. *Innovation in Organizations: Innovation Adoption in School Organizations.* New York: Elsevier.

Damanpour, Fariborz. 1996. "Organizational Complexity and Innovation: Develop-
    ing and Testing Multiple Contingency Models." *Management Science* 42, no. 5
    (May): 693–716.
Damanpour, Fariborz, and Shanthi Gopalakrishnan. 1998. "Theories of Organizational
    Structure and Innovation Adoption: The Role of Environmental Change." *Jour-
    nal of Engineering and Technology Management* 15, no. 1 (March): 1–24.
Dess, Gregory G., G. T. Lumpkin, and Jeffrey E. McGee. 1999. "Linking Corporate
    Entrepreneurship to Strategy, Structure, and Process: Suggested Research Direc-
    tions." *Entrepreneurship: Theory and Practice* 23 (March 22): 85–102.
Duncan, R. B. 1976. "The Ambidextrous Organization: Designing Dual Structures for
    Innovation." In *The Management of Organization Design: Strategies and Imple-
    mentation*, edited by Ralph H. Killman, Louis R. Pondy, and Dennis P. Slevin,
    167–88. New York: North-Holland.
Galunic, D. C., and K. M. Eisenhardt. 1994. "Renewing the Strategy-Structure-Per-
    formance Paradigm." In *Research in Organizational Behavior*, vol. 16, edited by
    Barry M. Staw and Larry L. Cummings, 215–55. Greenwich, CT: JAI Press.
Germain, Richard. 1996. "The Role of Context and Structure in Radical and Incre-
    mental Logistics Innovation Adoption." *Journal of Business Research* 35, no. 2
    (February): 117–27.
Gersick, Connie J. G. 1991. "Revolutionary Change Theories: A Multilevel Exploration
    of the Punctuated Equilibrium Paradigm." *Academy of Management Review* 16,
    no. 1 (January): 10–36.
Gibson, Cristina B., and Julian Birkinshaw. 2004. "The Antecedents, Consequences,
    and Mediating Role of Organizational Ambidexterity." *Academy of Management
    Journal* 47, no. 2 (April): 209–26. doi: 10.2307/20159573.
Gopalakrishnan, Shanthi. 2000. "Unraveling the Links between Dimensions of Innova-
    tion and Organizational Performance." *Journal of High Technology Management
    Research* 11, no. 1 (Spring): 137–53.
Grover, V., R. L. Purvis, and A. H. Segars. 2007. "Exploring Ambidextrous Innova-
    tion Tendencies in the Adoption of Telecommunication Technologies." *IEEE
    Transactions on Engineering Management* 54, no. 2: 268–85. doi: 10.1109/
    TEM.2007.893995.
Hage, Jerald, and Michael Aiken. 1967. "Program Change and Organizational Proper-
    ties: A Comparative Analysis." *American Journal of Sociology* 72, no. 5 (March):
    503–19.
Hambrick, Donald C. 1994. "Top Management Groups: A Conceptual Integration and
    Reconsideration of the 'Team' Label." In *Research in Organizational Behavior*,
    vol. 16, edited by Barry M. Staw and Larry L. Cummings, 171–213. Greenwich,
    CT: JAI Press.

————. 1995. "Fragmentation and the Other Problems CEOs Have with Their Top Management Teams." *California Management Review* 37, no. 3 (Spring): 110–27.

Hannan, Michael T., and John Freeman. 1984. "Structural Inertia and Organizational Change." *American Sociological Review* 49, no. 2 (April): 149–64.

He, Zi-Lin, and Poh-Kam Wong. 2004. "Exploration vs. Exploitation: An Empirical Test of the Ambidexterity Hypothesis." *Organization Science* 15, no. 4 (July/August): 481–94.

Jansen, Justin J. P., Michiel P. Tempelaar, Frans A. J. van den Bosch, and Henk W. Volberda. 2009. "Structural Differentiation and Ambidexterity: The Mediating Role of Integration Mechanisms." *Organization Science* 20, no. 4: 797–811.

Jantz, Ronald C. 2013. "Incremental and Radical Innovations—Survey," May 20, doi:10.7282/T37D2S88.

Kanter, Rosabeth Moss. 1983. *The Change Masters: Innovation and Entrepreneurship in the American Corporation.* New York: Simon & Schuster.

Kimberly, John R., and Michael J. Evanisko. 1981. "Organizational Innovation: The Influence of Individual, Organizational, and Contextual Factors on Hospital Adoption of Technological and Administrative Innovations." *Academy of Management Journal* 24, no. 4 (December 1): 689–713.

Lubatkin, Michael H., Zeki Simsek, Yan Ling, and John F. Veiga. 2006. "Ambidexterity and Performance in Small- to Medium-Sized Firms: The Pivotal Role of Top Management Team Behavioral Integration." *Journal of Management* 32, no. 5 (October): 646–72.

March, James G. 1991. "Exploration and Exploitation in Organizational Learning." *Organization Science* 2, no. 1: 71–87.

Noordegraaf, Mirko, and Rosemary Stewart. 2000. "Managerial Behavior Research in Private and Public Sectors: Distinctiveness, Disputes and Directions." *Journal of Management Studies* 37, no. 3 (May): 427–43.

Nord, Walter R., and Sharon Tucker. 1987. *Implementation of Routine and Radical Innovations.* Lexington, MA: Lexington Books.

O'Reilly III, Charles A., and Michael L. Tushman. 2004. "The Ambidextrous Organization." *Harvard Business Review*, April: 74–81.

————. 2008. "Ambidexterity as a Dynamic Capability: Resolving the Innovator's Dilemma." *Research in Organizational Behavior,* 28: 185–206. doi:10.1016/j.riob.2008.06.002.

Piao, Ming. 2010. "Thriving in the New: Implication of Exploration on Organizational Longevity." *Journal of Management* 36, no. 6: 1529–54.

Ravichandran, T. 2000. "Swiftness and Intensity of Administrative Innovation Adoption: An Empirical Study of TQM in Information Systems." *Decision Sciences* 31, no. 3 (September): 691–724.

Salge, T. O, and A. Vera. 2009. "Hospital Innovativeness and Organizational Performance: Evidence from English Public Acute Care." *Health Care Management Review* 34, no. 1: 54–67. doi:10.1097/01.HMR.0000342978.84307.80.

Sidhu, Jatinder S., Henk W. Volberda, and Harry R. Commandeur. 2004. "Exploring Exploration Orientation and Its Determinants: Some Empirical Evidence." *Journal of Management Studies* 41, no. 6 (September): 913–32.

Siegel, P. A., and Donald C. Hambrick. 1996. "Business Strategy and the Social Psychology of Top Management Teams." In *Advances in Strategic Management 13: The Embeddedness of Strategy*, edited by Joel A. C. Baum and Jane E. Dutton, 91–119. Greenwich, CT: JAI.

Simon, Julian L. 2003. *The Art of Empirical Investigation*. New Brunswick, NJ: Transaction Publishers.

Tushman, Michael L., and Charles A. O'Reilly III. 1996. Ambidextrous Organizations: Managing Evolutionary and Revolutionary Change. *California Management Review* 38, no. 4 (Summer): 8–30.

Tushman, Michael L., Wendy K. Smith, Robert Chapman Wood, George Westerman, and Charles A. O'Reilly III. 2002. "Innovation Streams and Ambidextrous Organizational Designs: On Building Dynamic Capabilities." Social Science Research Network Working Paper, December 2. http://web.mit.edu/sloan/osg-seminar/f02_docs/TushmanEtAl_2002.pdf.

Un, C. Annique. 2010. "An Empirical Multi-level Analysis for Achieving Balance between Incremental and Radical Innovations." *Journal of Engineering and Technology Management* 27, no. 1–2 (March–June): 1–19.

Van de Ven, Andrew H. 1986. "Central Problems in the Management of Innovation." *Management Science* 32, no. 5 (May): 590–607.

Walker, Richard M. 2008. "An Empirical Evaluation of Innovation Types and Organizational and Environmental Characteristics: Towards a Configuration Framework." *Journal of Public Administration Research and Theory* 18, no. 4: 591–615.

Warner, Rebecca M. 2013. *Applied Statistics: From Bivariate through Multivariate Techniques*. Thousand Oaks, CA: Sage.

Library Leadership:
A Shared Activity

IT IS PROBABLY OBVIOUS to most readers that a leader's preferences and choices can dramatically enhance or restrict an organization's performance and the ability to innovate. Empirical studies have demonstrated that the values and perceptions of leadership are influential predictors of innovation (Carmeli and Schaubroeck 2006; Rosing, Frese, and Bausch 2011).

In a study of leadership in human services organizations, Shin and McClomb (1998) found that innovation tended to be highest in organizations headed by top executives who were vision setters—leaders who searched for innovations, experimented with new concepts, and examined emerging social and economic trends. Mohr (1969) has identified essential leadership attributes for organizational change including a higher level of education, ability to cope with a high degree of uncertainty, and a willingness to communicate outside of the leader's local peer network. Van de Ven (1986, 601) states that institutional leadership is "critical in creating a cultural context that fosters innovation." More specifically, he states "creating these intra- and extra-organizational infrastructures in which innovation can flourish takes us directly to the strategic problem of innovation, which is institutional leadership." Based on their experience with the Baldridge model for innovation in academia, Furst-Bowe and Bauer (2007, 12) suggest that innovation and change "must be driven by individuals with line authority—presidents, vice-presidents, deans or department chairs." Yet, Hamel (2000, 61) notes that in most organizations "there are few individuals who can think holistically and concretely about new business concepts, or envision radical adjustments to existing business models."

In his book on innovation in nonprofits, Paul Light states that some scholars view leadership as "the sole factor in success." He further describes the role of the nonprofit leader as being the "principal architect of organizational life" (1998, 19–21). The "architectural" challenge for leaders is to create an organizational culture that is conducive to innovation and can be sustained over time. In this task, the university library leader will need to create an effective leadership team.

Leadership—A Shared Activity

The singular leader paradigm has dominated organizational behavior research for decades. Although a charismatic executive can lead an organization to success, this leadership style is highly dependent on personality and psychological traits that cannot easily be replicated. Scholars have argued that diverse and complementary skills are required in today's complex organizations, suggesting that leadership should become a shared activity (Hambrick 1995; Pearce and Conger 2003, xi–xii). In this model, the singular leader at the top of the organization shares authority with other members of the leadership team. As organizations grow more complex, it is increasingly difficult for a single individual to address all the leadership challenges. Friedrich and colleagues (2009) discuss a framework for understanding collective leadership where multiple individuals with complementary skills and knowledge share leadership roles. These researchers emphasize the dynamic aspects of the leadership process in which the specialized expertise of each member of the leadership team is selectively utilized.

This special expertise becomes even more important in managing the exploratory efforts that will become more prominent in the innovative library. Researchers and practitioners have long argued that the leadership team can promote creativity and the generation of ideas by utilizing different knowledge and experience to address difficult problems (Edmonson, Roberto, and Watkins 2003; Nadler 1996). Findings suggest a substantial benefit from collective leadership in the management of R&D teams. Hauschildt and Kirchmann (2001) demonstrated the benefit to R&D teams in having multiple leaders with different skill sets who act as champions. The champion connects the idea to the problem and helps push it through the stages of diffusion. Leadership champions can work together in supporting the research process, the adaptation of new technologies, and intergroup communication related to major new projects. Underlying these perspectives is the supposition that an effective leadership team, sharing leadership responsibilities with the singular leader, results in a more innovative library. In the end, the research library is better served by having a mix of leaders whose complementary skills and competencies—champion, critic, manager, technologist, mentor—can be utilized to orchestrate the necessary change in strategy and structure to create a more innovative culture.

Empirical Support for Behavioral Integration

These perspectives on shared leadership and the innovation process lead us directly to the importance of collaboration, information sharing, and joint decision making. These three behaviors combine into what Hambrick (1994, 188–89) has called "behavioral integration"—the degree to which the leadership engages in mutual and collective interaction.

The information-sharing aspect of behavioral integration contributes to ideas and new knowledge within the leadership team. Mom, Van Den Bosch, and Volberda (2007) found that horizontal knowledge flow in the management team, a form of sharing ideas, is positively related to the recipient's exploratory activities and has been found to enhance innovation and the creation of new knowledge. Carmeli and Schaubroeck (2006) note a behaviorally integrated top management team (TMT)[14] is characterized by intense interaction that produces open information exchange and collaboration-based decisions. These TMT decisions are typically more complex than those encountered in other work groups. Carmeli and Schaubroeck examined the impact of behavioral integration on organizational decline using a sample of 116 TMTs from various industries. They found that behavioral integration was negatively related to organizational decline (i.e., more behavioral integration results in less decline) and was positively related to the perceived quality of strategic decisions. In a sur-

---

[14] The top management team is the relatively small group of influential leaders and managers at the top of the organization (Hambrick 1995). In this text, the phrase *top management team* is considered synonymous with *leadership team*.

vey of teams from 96 service organizations, Carmeli (2008) found that TMT behavioral integration is positively associated with both human resource performance and economic performance.

Scholars have examined various aspects of the leadership team that are closely related to behavioral integration. Marion (2012, 468) and Kazanjian and Drazin (2012) discuss the role of leadership in collective creativity, a process that can lead to the dispersion of ideas throughout an organization. Damanpour and Aravind (2012, 503) report that internal communication and "a climate conducive to the dispersion of ideas across the organization" were positively related to innovation in two waves of meta-analyses. Uhl-Bien and colleagues (2007) coined the phrase "enabling leadership," where the formal leaders of the organization are particularly well suited to stimulate creativity because of their networks, access to resources, and authority. A more behaviorally integrated leadership team may be able to carry out this enabling leadership, resulting in an organization generating more ideas that lead to improved innovativeness. Talke, Salomo, and Rost (2010) found that TMT diversity in functional background, experience, and values can have a strong impact on the decision to focus on an innovative strategy. These research results demonstrate the benefits to the organization of a more integrated leadership team.

Supporting the Stages of Diffusion

Library leadership with different skills and expertise can facilitate key actions in each of the stages in the innovation diffusion process (figure 3.1). If innovativeness is to be a part of organizational life, leaders will need to provide support for an idea as it moves from inception to successful implementation. In the initiation stage, the leader must help gather new ideas and insure that the best ideas are given due attention and discussion before being tabled or discarded. Providing psychological protection to those who might otherwise be reluctant to share unorthodox ideas is crucial at this early stage. In the innovation adoption stage, it is the leader's responsibility to bring the management team together to discuss and arrive at a decision to proceed with implementation of the innovation. In most organizations, decisions do not emanate unilaterally from the singular leader at the top of the organization. Rather, leaders and managers participate in the decision process by constantly communicating and making tradeoffs between meeting current needs and developing capabilities for the future. One of the most important leadership responsibilities following the adoption decision is to communicate the decision to the organization.

It is in the third diffusion stage where scholars (Klein and Sorra 1996) have identified "implementation failure" as a major reason that an organization does not reap the full benefits of an innovation. To successfully implement a major new innovation, leaders must provide the necessary resources and also create the environment in which the implementation team can focus on process, quality, and development schedules.

Behavioral Integration of the ARL Leadership Teams

In order to capture the behavioral integration construct in the ARL innovation study, team members were asked to respond to statements regarding their team's collaboration, information sharing, and decision making.[15] A sample statement requiring agreement on a nine-point Likert scale was as follows: "Team members usually let each other know when their actions affect another team member's work."

As noted in the regression model (figure 4.2), it was hypothesized that behavioral integration would be positively associated with innovation performance in the research library (Hypothesis H1). Behavioral integration of the leadership team was strongly correlated with innovation performance ($r = 0.33$, $p < .01$, $n = 50$) as illustrated in the bivariate correlation of figure 5.1. Although there are a few outliers, the general pattern indicates that a research library with a more integrated leadership team will be more innovative. After controlling for size (based on FTE) and type of institution (public or private) in the regression model, behavioral integration remained positive and significant, suggesting that behavioral integration remains strongly impacting after statistically removing the effects of library size and the type of institution.

The rationale for this result originates with the leadership team's ability to collaborate and to share information. In joint decision mak-

---

[15] See questions 1–9 on the innovation survey (Jantz 2013).

FIGURE 5.1
Correlation of Behavioral Integration with Innovation Performance (*N* = 50)

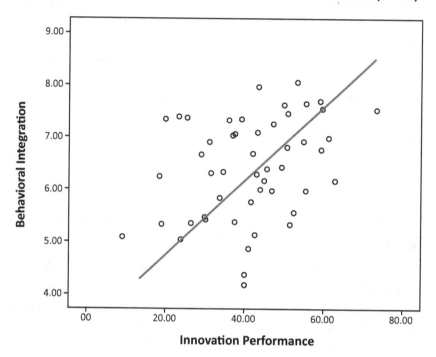

ing, the TMT becomes aware of the decision made by the team and the complete team is more able to support the innovation throughout the diffusion stages and introduction to the user community. Information sharing can result in new ideas that can ultimately become innovations. Leaders in a behaviorally integrated team are not likely to withdraw into their own domains where incremental improvements to existing services are the prevailing mode of innovation. This more integrated behavior is especially significant in relation to radical innovations and bringing about major change in the organization. The less integrated team will have difficulty embracing new strategic imperatives and formulating responses to these imperatives. Members of these less integrated teams are accustomed to running their own show and will have difficulty adapting to new environmental imperatives (Hambrick 1994, 200).

Making Decisions

A more integrated leadership team is better able to commit to a new strategy, a major new initiative, or a change in organizational structure. Thus, decisions regarding these actions—their clarity, how achieved, and how communicated—are a critical element in the life of the library. As indicated in stage two of the diffusion model (figure 3.1), the leadership team must reach a decision to adopt an innovation before proceeding with implementation. It is useful to reflect on how decisions are made in the library and examine the research literature in this important area. What is surprising in the institutional environment, and specifically the research library, is how little effort is spent on examining the effectiveness of the decision process and how it might be improved. Yet, "it is in the decision process that everything comes together" (Drucker 1990, 121).

In studying the decision process in academic libraries, Mash (2010, 30–39) has nicely summarized the five major decision models. As we can see from the various decision models, making a decision in the institutional environment is a complex process. The decision process might be *bureaucratic*, in which decisions are made by actors who have formal roles and within formal structures. Decision power derives from having a recognized title and being the leader of a unit in the library. However, in the *political* model, decision power can emanate from informal, local groups and from individuals with different viewpoints and opinions. Many in the library might suggest that the *collegial* model is most dominant, in which organization members have equal status and where full participation and consensus is the objective. It is interesting that researchers consider the *rational* model as one that does not portray what actually happens in the decision process. In reality, leaders involved in a decision process are often confronted with enormous complexity and many possible outcomes such that a rational decision process becomes unlikely. In these situations, leaders fall back on behavioral traits in order to make a decision (Hambrick and Manson 1984).

Aspects of each of these models are encountered in the decision-making process, suggesting that the fifth model, the *garbage can* model, might be the most appropriate. In a seminal paper, Cohen, March, and Olsen (1972) describe the garbage can model and propose that it applies in organized hierarchies such as universities and other public and educational institutions. In this process, a decision opportunity can be viewed as "a garbage can in which various kinds of problems and solutions are dumped" (Cohen, March and Olsen, 1972, 2). In studying the garbage can model, Daft and Becker (1978, 166–75) report that decisions in high schools do not follow an orderly process but are outcomes of relatively independent streams of events. In the library, as the leadership team confronts a decision opportunity, these streams include unclear or unstated preferences, uncertainty about how to prioritize opportunities, and fluid participation in the proposed project based on individual perceptions of responsibility.

Although the garbage can model has a pejorative ring, it is apparent in the ARL study that leaders in the more innovative libraries were able to make decisions about proceeding with risky projects. Although the study did not provide insight into the actual decision process, the analysis examined the factor *decision awareness*, which was based on the library leadership team arriving at a consensus regarding the decision to implement an innovation.

Decision Awareness

In the diffusion process of figure 3.1, the decision stage focuses on the choice to implement or not to implement an innovation. In the ARL study, library leaders were presented with a list of 32 innovations and asked to indicate if their institution had made a decision to implement the cited innovation (See "Research Library Innovations"—appendix B).[16] The *decision awareness* variable was created based on whether the library leadership team had arrived at a consensus regarding the decision to implement. Decision awareness was identified as an enabler variable, and the regression analysis demonstrated a significant and positive relationship between decision awareness and innovation performance. There are several explanations for why decision awareness has a significant and positive impact on innovation performance.

First, one might expect that an integrated leadership team would be more aware of decisions regarding innovative projects. In fact, decision awareness is highly correlated with behavioral integration ($r = .38, p < .01$, $n = 50$). However, decision awareness also represents a different aspect of the leadership team. In most complex social organizations, it is difficult to establish clarity about a decision. Leaders may leave a meeting with quite

---

[16] On the ARL survey, two questions were posed for each of 32 innovations. See questions 33–96 (Jantz 2013).

different views about whether or not a decision has been made to implement an innovation. The decision awareness predictor provides insight as to how well an organization can establish clarity regarding a decision and how effectively it can communicate the decision within the team and to the larger organization. Secondly, the impact of decision awareness on innovation is quite obvious. For innovations to succeed, leaders in the library must provide their full support. An innovation will not garner much support if organizational members are not aware that a decision has been made. Uncertainty in the leadership team regarding the decision to implement will surely affect aspects of the implementation process such as obtaining resources, especially if those resources are to be drawn from several different units. Further, if there are political differences within the team, uncertainty about a decision provides a convenient excuse for not supporting the innovation. The bivariate correlation of decision awareness with innovation performance is illustrated in figure 5.2 ($r = 0.42$, $p < .01$, n

FIGURE 5.2
Correlation of Decision Awareness with Innovation Performance ($N = 50$)

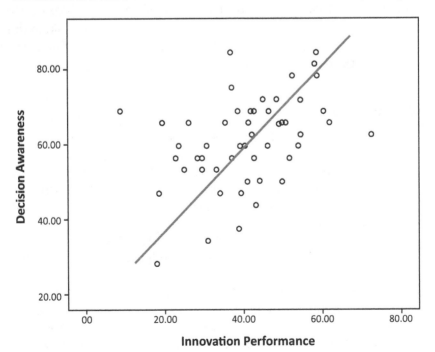

= 50). The scatter plot indicates quite clearly that more decision awareness among the leadership team contributes to a more innovative library.

Conclusion

From the empirical results, behavioral integration and decision awareness of the leadership team clearly have a very positive impact on the ability of the research library to innovate. Of course, a major challenge for the library leadership team is how to become more integrated. The diversity of skills, demographics, and niche specialties within the team can complicate communication and the integration process (Cox, Pearce, and Perry 2003, 50). Fragmentation of the team, destructive rivalries, groupthink, and the lack of trust can render the team ineffective (Walker 2008). The conflicting signals emanating from various constituencies and the external environment are susceptible to multiple interpretations and can create confusion within the organization (Hambrick 1995). However, these conflicts and tensions are part of a more innovative culture, one in which the singular leader—the director or university librarian—will be challenged to seek a balance within the team between content-rich collaborations and a more harmonious team that veers toward groupthink. In this role, the singular leader does, in fact, become the architect of organizational life in the research library.

References

Carmeli, Abraham. 2008. "Top Management Team Behavioral Integration and the Performance of Service Organizations." *Group and Organization Management* 33, no. 6 (December): 712–35. doi:10.1177/1059601108325696.

Carmeli, Abraham, and John Schaubroeck. 2006. "Top Management Team Behavioral Integration, Decision Quality, and Organizational Decline." *Leadership Quarterly* 17, no. 5 (October): 441–53.

Cohen, Michael D., James G. March, and Johan P. Olsen. 1972. "A Garbage Can Model of Organizational Choice." *Administrative Science Quarterly* 17, no. 1 (March): 1–25.

Cox, Jonathan F., Craig L. Pearce, and Monica L. Perry. 2003. "Toward a Model of Shared Leadership and Distributed Influence in the Innovation Process: How Shared Leadership Can Enhance New Product Development Team Dynamics and Effectiveness." In *Shared Leadership: Reframing the Hows and Whys of*

Leadership, edited by Craig L. Pearce and Jay A. Conger, 48–76. London: Sage Publications.

Daft, Richard L., and Selwyn W. Becker. 1978. *Innovation in Organizations: Innovation Adoption in School Organizations.* New York: Elsevier.

Damanpour, Fariborz, and Deepa Aravind. 2012. "Organizational Structure and Innovation Revisited: From Organic to Ambidextrous Structure." In *Handbook of Organizational Creativity*, edited by Michael D. Mumford, 483–513. Waltham, MA: Academic Press.

Drucker, Peter F. 1990. *Managing the Nonprofit Organization: Practices and Principles.* New York: HarperCollins.

Edmondson, Amy C., Michael A. Roberto, and Michael D. Watkins. 2003. "A Dynamic Model of Top Management Team Effectiveness: Managing Unstructured Task Streams." *Leadership Quarterly* 14, no. 3 (June): 297–325.

Friedrich, Tamara L., William B. Vessey, Matthew J. Schuelke, Gregory A. Ruark, and Michael D. Mumford. 2009. "A Framework for Understanding Collective Leadership: The Selective Utilization of Leader and Team Expertise within Networks." *Leadership Quarterly* 20, no. 6 (December): 933–58.

Furst-Bowe, Julie A., and Roy A. Bauer. 2007. "Application of the Baldrige Model for Innovation in Higher Education." *New Directions for Higher Education* no. 137 (Spring): 5–14.

Hambrick, Donald C. 1994. "Top Management Groups: A Conceptual Integration and Reconsideration of the 'Team' Label." In *Research in Organizational Behavior*, vol. 16, edited by Barry M. Staw and Larry L. Cummings, 171–213. Greenwich, CT: JAI Press.

———. 1995. "Fragmentation and the Other Problems CEOs Have with Their Top Management Teams." *California Management Review* 37, no. 3 (Spring): 110–27.

Hambrick, Donald C., and P. A. Manson. 1984. "Upper Echelons: The Organization as a Reflection of Its Top Managers." *Academy of Management Review* 9, no. 2 (April): 193–206.

Hamel, Gary. 2000. *Leading the Revolution.* Boston: Harvard Business School Press.

Hauschildt, J., and E. Kirchmann. 2001. "Teamwork for Innovation—The 'Troika' of Promoters." *R&D Management* 31, no. 1: 41–49.

Jantz, Ronald C. 2013. "Incremental and Radical Innovations—Survey," May 20, doi:10.7282/T37D2S88.

Kazanjian, Robert K., and Robert Drazin. 2012. "Organizational Learning, Knowledge Management and Creativity." In *Handbook of Organizational Creativity*, edited by Michael D. Mumford, 547–68, Waltham, MA: Academic Press.

Klein, Katherine J., and Joann Speer Sorra. 1996. "The Challenge of Innovation Implementation." *Academy of Management Review* 21, no. 4 (October): 1055–83.

Light, Paul C. 1998. *Sustaining Innovation: Creating Nonprofit and Government Organizations That Innovate Naturally.* San Francisco: Jossey-Bass.

Marion, Russ. 2012. "Leadership of Creativity: Entity-Based, Relational, and Complexity Perspectives." In *Handbook of Organizational Creativity,* edited by Michael D. Mumford, 457–79, Waltham, MA: Academic Press.

Mast, S. David. 2010. *Decision Making in the Absence of Certainty: A Study in the Context of Technology and the Construction of the 21st Century Academic Library.* Chicago: Association of College and Research Libraries.

Mohr, Lawrence B. 1969. "Determinants of Innovation in Organizations." *American Political Science Review* 63, no. 1 (March): 111–26.

Mom, Tom J. M., Frans A. J. Van Den Bosch, and Henk W. Volberda. 2007. "Investigating Managers' Exploration and Exploitation Activities: The Influence of Top-Down, Bottom-Up, and Horizontal Knowledge Inflows." *Journal of Management Studies* 44, no. 6 (September): 910–31.

Nadler, David A. 1996. "Managing the Team at the Top." *Strategy and Business* 2: 42–51.

Pearce, Craig L., and Jay A. Conger, eds. 2003. *Shared Leadership: Reframing the Hows and Whys of Leadership.* London: Sage Publications.

Rosing, Kathrin, Michael Frese, and Andreas Bausch. 2011. "Explaining the Heterogeneity of the Leadership-Innovation Relationship: Ambidextrous Leadership." *Leadership Quarterly* 22, no. 5 (October): 956–74.

Shin, Junseob, and George E. McClomb. 1998. "Top Executive Leadership and Organizational Innovation." *Administration in Social Work* 22, no. 3: 1–21. doi:10.1300/J147v22n03_01.

Talke, Katrin, Sören Salomo, and Katja Rost. 2010. "How Top Management Team Diversity Affects Innovativeness and Performance via the Strategic Choice to Focus on Innovation Fields." *Research Policy* 39, no. 7 (September): 907–18.

Uhl-Bien, Mary, Russ Marion, and Bill McKelvey. 2007. "Complexity Leadership Theory: Shifting Leadership from the Industrial Age to the Knowledge Era." *Leadership Quarterly* 18, no. 4 (August): 298–318.

Van de Ven, Andrew H. 1986. "Central Problems in the Management of Innovation." *Management Science* 32, no. 5 (May): 590–607.

Walker, Richard M. 2008. "An Empirical Evaluation of Innovation Types and Organizational and Environmental Characteristics: Towards a Configuration Framework." *Journal of Public Administration Research and Theory* 18, no. 4: 591–615.

Chapter 6

The Flexible Organization and Library Culture

TUSHMAN AND O'REILLY (1996, 8) pose a rhetorical question: "Why is anything but incremental change often so difficult for the most successful organizations?" Their answer is that organizations and managers must become ambidextrous. This balancing act and the tension between exploring new opportunities while also supporting and improving existing services represents one of the most difficult challenges that a leader will face (O'Reilly and Tushman 2004). Finding an appropriate balance between these activities is made more difficult since the same issues surface at different levels—the individual, the group, and the organization (March 1991).

Organizational life will be quite different for the leader of an ambidextrous library. There is more risk in the search for new knowledge and the use of unfamiliar technologies. A major new innovation may not produce results until some time in the distant future. Tradeoffs will have to be made between investing in the support of traditional library services and the unproven new service. New organizational structures and different skill sets will be required. As a result, the demands on the library will always be somewhat in conflict, suggesting that reaching decisions will be more controversial and time-consuming. The conundrum for leaders is that the success of existing services brings inertia and creates a more conservative, risk-averse culture.

Why would library leaders initiate a risky venture when feedback from stakeholders is largely positive, and why would a manager de-emphasize or eliminate an existing service to fund a totally new service? Responses to these difficult questions will be necessary to create a more innovative culture, as Jesse Shera (1966, 95) recognized some 50 years ago, suggesting that the librarian "must be both critic and architect—destroyer of that which is obsolete and builder of his own future."

The Ambidextrous Organization—Exploration and Exploitation

The concept of ambidexterity is grounded in a strategy to simultaneously pursue both evolutionary and revolutionary initiatives. According to March (1991), finding a balance between these types of initiatives is particularly difficult because of the inherent organizational conflicts that emerge from exploration and exploitation activities.[17] Exploitation is defined here as the enhancement and refinement of existing library services, whereas exploration results in new knowledge and the development of totally new services. Typically, exploitation will result in incremental innovations while exploration can produce the more radical innovation. The essence of exploitation is the leveraging of existing knowledge, skills, and services in the library. There is near consensus in the research literature that organizations must excel at both exploration and exploitation in order to survive and thrive (Cao, Simsek, and Zhang 2010; Gupta, Smith, and Shalley 2006; Heavey 2009; O'Reilly and Tushman 2008). On the other hand, too little of either exploration or exploitation can reduce performance (Greve 2007). Exploration without an appropriate level of exploitation can result in underdeveloped ideas that never mature into fully realized innovations. Undue emphasis on exploitation, however, will sacrifice the future.

Examples in the library will illustrate both the organizational and technical characteristics of exploration and exploitation activities. Audiovisual materials have been available in libraries since the 1940s (Shane 1940). The exploratory work of Shane culminated in a proposal to launch

---

[17] We use March's (1991) vocabulary in which exploratory activities result in new knowledge and possibly radical innovations whereas exploitation focuses on using existing knowledge to produce incremental innovations.

a new service for the library to manage audiovisual materials. In order to convince skeptical and reluctant librarians that this was a good idea, Shane suggested that AV aids are themselves "books of a kind" (143). He also outlined the types of AV materials and the complexity of the new service, including the purchasing and support of complicated equipment. Shane explained how existing library skills for selection, classification, and cataloging could be leveraged or, in terms of March's vocabulary, exploited. In the early 1940s, the introduction of AV materials into the library was quite radical. However, traditional library skills facilitated implementation, illustrating the important balance and complementary aspects of exploration and exploitation.

Today, audiovisual materials are readily available in the research library. However, for most users, the AV experience still remains largely sequential—start at the beginning of the recording and listen or view until the user information need has been resolved. More recently, major improvements to AV access have resulted from library research and development. For example, software-based video annotation capabilities enable the user to identify, annotate, and view video clips, thereby allowing more direct access to relevant information and significantly enhancing the user experience. The annotation enables access to any segment of the AV resource without fast-forwarding, opening up the possibilities for innovative classroom instruction (Agnew, Mills, and Maher 2010).

Speech recognition, the translation of speech to text, offers the possibility of even more radical AV innovations. Continuing to enhance the AV user experience, librarians might investigate emerging technologies (Lin and Zhang 2008) to do speaker-independent automatic speech recognition. This technology can render a video or sound file as text, with appropriate time stamps for each word. The automatically created, text-based surrogate for the video can be full-text searched with a capability for the user to jump into the video at any point, using the time stamp.

This progression from introducing AV materials into the library, to enhancing the AV service, and, finally, to offering advanced capabilities demonstrates the positive interplay of exploratory and exploitative activities and the importance of these activities coexisting in the ambidextrous organization.

Empirical Support for Ambidexterity

Innovation studies have demonstrated the impact of ambidexterity on organizations with characteristics similar to those of the research library. Researchers have used different theoretical frameworks to study ambidexterity, including the ambidextrous orientation, knowledge strategy, the learning organization, and organizational adaptation. Bierly and Daly (2007) used the knowledge-based view to examine small to medium-size enterprises (SMEs) that are frequently more resource-constrained compared to their larger counterparts. In a broad sampling of different types of SMEs, these researchers found that exploration is positively related to firm performance, while exploitation is positive only up to a point, at which more exploitation leads to a reduced performance. The research of Corso and Pellegrini (2007) provides insight into how an organization might become ambidextrous with less risk, suggesting that exploration can result in a series of incremental innovations rather than a single, more radical and discontinuous innovation. In this approach, the organization increases its knowledge base through exploration, but minimizes risk by gradually introducing new capabilities.

For research libraries to continue exploitation and deliver high-quality service to their clients, they must have well-developed processes. However, Benner and Tushman (2003) offer a cautionary proposition. Although process focus can result in improved efficiency and quality, process management techniques trigger internal biases that favor predictability at the expense of exploration and more innovation. In a related observation, Greve (2007) notes that the momentum that organizations develop from their daily routines makes repetition more likely than novelty and gives greater rewards to short-term actions. These two research reports suggest that a process focus must be appropriately moderated depending on context. The more exploratory work will have looser processes and unfamiliar language and will likely experience more unsuccessful projects than the refinements introduced through exploitation and incremental innovation.

Ambidexterity in ARL Libraries

For the *ambidextrous orientation* in the library, this study used a scale developed by Lubatkin and colleagues (2006). Library leaders responded to statements that enabled them to express their views on their organization's ability to conduct both exploratory and exploitative activities. For exploration, a sample survey statement was "Your library bases its success on its ability to explore and develop new technologies and services." For exploitation, a sample statement was "Your library continuously improves the reliability of its products and services." Library leaders responded to these statements by indicating their agreement or disagreement on a nine-point Likert scale. These responses from leaders created a picture of the organization's current status and strategy that focused on the ability of the library to conduct both exploratory and exploitative activities.

From the regression model of figure 4.2, it was hypothesized that an ambidextrous orientation would be positively related to the innovation performance of the library. The regression results did, in fact, demonstrate that a more ambidextrous orientation leads to improved library innovation performance and the ability to implement both radical and incremental innovations. These results are also evident in the bivariate correlation of the ambidextrous orientation with innovation performance ($r = 0.42$,

FIGURE 6.1

Correlation of Ambidextrous Orientation with Innovation Performance ($N = 50$)

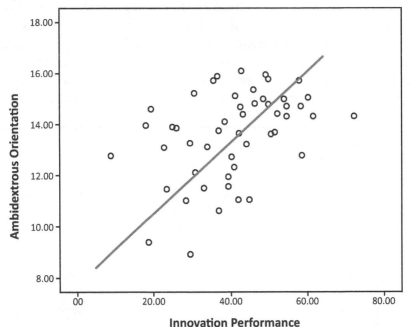

$p < .01$, $n = 50$), as illustrated in figure 6.1. The figure clearly indicates that the more ambidextrous library has better innovation performance. Therefore, hypothesis H2a, which proposed that the ambidextrous orientation of the library would be positively related to innovation performance, was supported.

Although the ambidexterity-innovation performance finding is important in itself, the relationship of senior team integration to the ambidextrous orientation holds even more promise for the library.

The Mediation Effect

One of the most significant findings of the ARL study was the mediation effect that occurred between integration of the leadership team, the ambidexterity of the organization, and innovation performance. The statistical concept of mediation involves a hypothesis about the relationship between three variables. A common example for illustrative purposes involves the effects of age and weight gain on blood pressure in humans. Increased age can cause weight gain and weight gain can result in an increase in blood pressure. The effects of age are transmitted or "mediated" by weight to impact blood pressure (Warner 2013, 646–47).

For mediation to occur in the ARL study, it must be shown that there is a possible causal sequence among three variables where X_1 (*behavioral integration*) causes X_2 (*ambidextrous orientation*) and then X_2 (*ambidextrous orientation*) causes X_3 (*innovation performance*). For the ARL study, the mediation hypothesis is that the effects of behavioral integration will be transmitted by an ambidextrous orientation and have an impact on innovation

FIGURE 6.2
The Mediating Effect

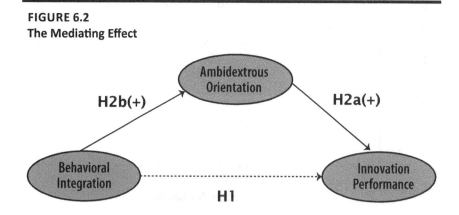

performance. This hypothesized relationship for the ARL study requires that both H2a and H2b be demonstrated, as illustrated in figure 6.2.

Intuitively, behavioral integration of the senior team would likely be developed well before there is evidence of the more sophisticated ambidextrous strategy, thus making a causal relationship between behavioral integration and an ambidextrous orientation possible. The rationale for this observation is that simultaneously supporting both exploratory and exploitative activities represents a new experience for the research library and it is likely to cause conflict as the leadership team debates the tradeoffs between supporting new services and continuing to support traditional services. New organizational structures and revised strategies resulting in more ambidexterity will challenge existing authority and embedded power structures. A more integrated and collaborative senior team will be able to cope with these challenges better than the less integrated team. Thus, as required for mediation, the integration of the senior team would be developed well before the more challenging ambidextrous orientation.

FIGURE 6.3
Correlation between Ambidextrous Orientation and Behavioral Integration (*N* = 50)

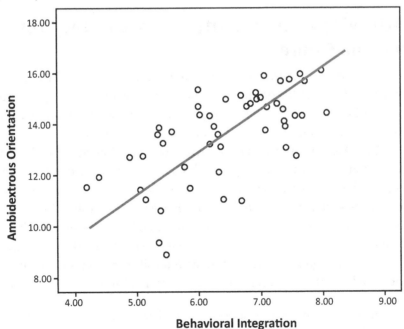

In the mediation model (figure 6.2), it was hypothesized (H2b) that the independent variable, *behavioral integration,* would influence the mediator, *ambidextrous orientation,* which in turn would impact the dependent variable (H2a), *innovation performance.* Strong support for hypothesis H2b is demonstrated in the bivariate correlation between *ambidextrous orientation* and *behavioral integration* ($r = 0.63, p < .01, n = 50$) as illustrated in figure 6.3.

In the mediation analysis,[18] hypotheses H2a and H2b were supported, and the direct impact of behavioral integration on innovation performance became insignificant, indicating that the ambidextrous orientation did in fact mediate the relationship between behavioral integration and innovation performance. As a result, the mediation effect explains a significant part of the total effect of behavioral integration on innovation performance. The bottom line: library leadership teams who have found ways to collaborate, share information, and participate in joint decision making *and* have created a strategy that simultaneously supports current services while also exploring new services are likely to be much more innovative than their peer institutions that have less integrated teams and are less ambidextrous.

Achieving Ambidexterity—Balancing the Present and the Future

Most libraries are quite good at maintaining and refining their existing services. However, becoming more ambidextrous suggests a significantly new outlook in which leaders engage in a balancing act, paying attention to existing capabilities while also pursuing radically new services.

The ARL study results have shown how a more integrated senior team with an ambidextrous strategy can dramatically improve the innovativeness of the research library. Leaders may choose different organizational strategies to achieve ambidexterity. For example, exploration may be conducted in a unit that is structurally separated from those units that are conducting the daily business of the library. Benner and Tushman (2003, 247) provide a good description of the requisite organizational structures for ambidexterity: "the exploratory units are small and decentralized, with

---

[18] For readers who would like to explore the detailed statistical analysis, please see the author's dissertation (Jantz 2013).

loose cultures and processes, the exploitation units are larger and more centralized, with tight cultures and processes." The exploratory units may have their own strategies with quite different cultures and are similar to the classic R&D organization. As one example, Grover, Purvis, and Segars (2007) found that organizational configurations for doing incremental innovation and creating radical innovations do, in fact, exist simultaneously in the same organization. However, a significant managerial challenge remains in finding ways to stimulate communication across dissimilar units and to integrate research results into mainstream library services.

Recent research (Piao 2010; Raisch et al. 2009) has delved into the complexity of organizational ambidexterity and sheds light on the choices and challenges that leaders will face in becoming ambidextrous. Raisch and colleagues explored central tensions in how ambidexterity might be implemented in an organization, whereas Piao examined the effects of the temporal separation of exploration and exploitation. The path to ambidexterity may be quite different for each research library, and the analysis here builds on Raisch's research by examining the alternatives that a library might pursue.

Structural Differentiation versus Integration

Exploration activities can be partitioned into separate units (differentiation) or integrated in the units that provide existing services. Undertaking exploratory work in a separate unit helps the library in growing new knowledge and competencies and minimizes the negative effects of a process-oriented organization on exploration.

The organizational structure is only a first step or precondition for ambidexterity; it is the processes by which the units are integrated that result in ambidexterity. This structural challenge exemplifies the importance of a more integrated senior team (Smith and Tushman 2005) and how the dual constructs of *behavioral integration* and *ambidextrous orientation* work together. Jansen and colleagues (2009, 798) note that senior team integration contributes to "balanced resource allocation and establishes cross-fertilization across exploratory and exploitative activities."

The structural approach does not have to be a static one in which an organizational structure is established and remains intact for years. New structures and configurations are needed more frequently in order to meet the demands of a dynamic environment. Many of these demands originate with the parent institution, including curriculum changes, financial management, new modes of information delivery, and evolving managerial emphases (Budd 2012, 337). Raisch and colleagues (2009, 688) note that organizations must continuously "reconfigure their activities," adapting to rapid changes in both internal and external environments.

Organizational separation into exploratory and exploitation units allows for different processes and cultures, but also creates difficulties in cross-unit communication and integrating research results into the mainstream of the organization. This organizational separation can be managed through a tightly integrated senior team. In a case study of 15 business units in nine different industries, O'Reilly and Tushman (2004) found that 90 percent of the ambidextrous organizations achieved their goals. According to these researchers, organizations do not have to abandon their current products and services while also pursuing breakthrough initiatives—the secret is to create organizationally distinct units that are tightly integrated by the senior leadership team.

Contextual Ambidexterity

In contrast to structural ambidexterity, the contextual approach does not assume separate units to support exploration and exploitation activities (Gibson and Birkinshaw 2004). In the contextual approach, all members of the organization are empowered to be innovative and to use their own judgment as to when more exploration is warranted versus following standard organizational practices. Gibson and Birkinshaw found that ambidexterity thus defined is positively related to organizational performance. In a related study, Bierly and Daly (2007, 495) note "these exceptional firms possess the seemingly contradictory skills and competencies of both [exploration and exploitation], and have subcultures within the organization that support each approach." These contradictory skills can be supported through various management practices. Trust, employee training, and management flexibility are key ingredients for this type of ambidexterity to succeed. Although the contextual approach will gradually build the more innovative culture, it will require a less hierarchical and more organic structure where leaders are comfortable with and confident in their organizational members pursuing the right course of action.

Temporal Separation

How much exploratory work should be conducted in parallel or simultaneously with exploitative activities? Piao (2010) examined the overlap between exploration and exploitation, hypothesizing that the overlap is related to the longevity of for-profit firms. Too much exploratory work can reduce the benefits from exploitative activities, while too much exploitation jeopardizes the future by not creating the new knowledge and ideas that are needed for innovation. *Longevity* is a term that is used in the for-profit sector in which firms fall victim to competition and poor management practices. The corresponding phenomenon in research libraries is organizational decline in which libraries continue to put undue emphasis on exploiting current services while ignoring the future. If a library, however, invests heavily in research, possibly by taking on too many grant-funded projects, the support and improvement of current services is likely to suffer. Piao's hypothesis that a U-shaped relationship exists between firm longevity and the overlap of exploration and exploitation was supported, suggesting that those organizations that have moderate overlap are likely to be more successful, resulting in organizational

FIGURE 6.4
Balance between Exploitation and Exploration and Organizational Advancement

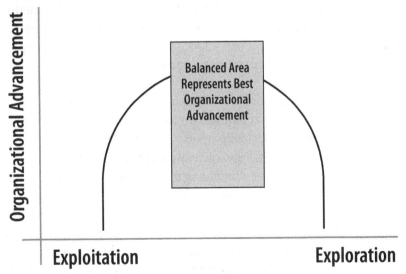

advancement. Based on this research, we can speculate that a U-shaped relationship for libraries is most appropriate, where a balance between exploitation and exploration results in organizational advancement, as represented in figure 6.4.

For library leaders, there are two important results from these observations: (*a*) the investment in exploratory and exploitative projects must be explicitly managed to achieve the right amount of balance and overlap, and (*b*) although exploration and exploitation priorities can cause tension in the organization, these activities are also complementary where expertise and knowledge flow in both directions.

Conclusion

Ultimately, the task of becoming more ambidextrous is one of changing library culture. Assessments and reviews of library culture are seldom undertaken (Budd 2012, 68; Shepstone and Currie 2008). Over the past 100 years or so, the norms of the library profession and the associated values, beliefs, and principles have acted as an "iron cage" restricting innovation (DiMaggio and Powell 1983). Tushman and O'Reilly (1996) describe this phenomenon as "cultural inertia" resulting, in part, from the success of current products and services. These forces of inertia can be persistent and very strong.

When an organization is confronted with a dynamic and sometimes turbulent environment, the embedded culture can become a barrier to success. McDonald and Thomas (2006, 4) provide just one example of missed opportunities resulting from a traditional culture:

> Our services and policies are equally limiting, seemingly guided more by fear of litigation than any other factor. Privacy and intellectual property are more important than ever in a digital age, certainly, but libraries protect both to the point of eliminating many capabilities modern technologies otherwise make possible.

But this change to a more innovative culture is not just a shift or minor adjustment. The ambidextrous orientation and the ability to both explore and exploit suggests that the transformation should focus on developing multiple library cultures. Tushman and O'Reilly (1996) paint a picture of a layered culture in which there are common values shared by everyone in the organization—transparency, the sharing of information, and trust. This top layer provides the "glue" that holds the differing subcultures together. At the same time, different units will have widely varying subcultures that are more specific to their unique roles and objectives in the library. Librarians and staff will need to understand the ambidextrous strategy and this cultural shift, requiring leaders to clearly and repeatedly communicate how exploration and exploitation can coexist in the same organization and become mutually beneficial.

References

Agnew, G., C. M. Mills, and C. A. Maher. 2010. "VMCAnalytic: Developing a Collaborative Video Analysis Tool for Education Faculty and Practicing Educators." In *Proceedings of the 43rd Hawaii International Conference on System Sciences (HICSS-43)*, edited by Ralph H. Sprague, Jr., 10 pages. Los Alamitos, CA: IEEE Computer Society. doi:10.1109/HICSS.2010.438.

Benner, Mary J., and Michael L. Tushman. 2003. "Exploration, Exploitation, and Process Management: The Productivity Dilemma Revisited." *Academy of Management Review* 28, no. 2 (April): 238–56.

Bierly III, Paul E., and Paula S. Daly. 2007. "Alternative Knowledge Strategies, Competitive Environment, and Organizational Performance in Small Manufacturing Firms." *Entrepreneurship Theory and Practice* 31, no. 4 (July): 493–516.

Budd, John M. 2012. *The Changing Academic Library: Operations, Culture, Environments*. Chicago: Association of College and Research Libraries.

Cao, Qing, Zeki Simsek, and Hongping Zhang. 2010. "Modelling the Joint Impact of the CEO and the TMT on Organizational Ambidexterity." *Journal of Management Studies* 47, no. 7 (November): 1272–96.

Corso, Mariano, and Luisa Pellegrini. 2007. "Continuous and Discontinuous Innovation: Overcoming the Innovator Dilemma." *Creativity and Innovation Management* 16, no. 4 (December): 333–47.

DiMaggio, Paul J., and Walter W. Powell. 1983. "The Iron Cage Revisited: Institutional Isomorphism and Collective Rationality in Organizational Fields." *American Sociological Review* 48, no. 2: 147–60.

Gibson, Cristina B., and Julian Birkinshaw. 2004. "The Antecedents, Consequences, and Mediating Role of Organizational Ambidexterity." *Academy of Management Journal* 47, no. 2 (April): 209–26.

Greve, Henrich R. 2007. "Exploration and Exploitation in Product Innovation." *Industrial and Corporate Change* 16, no. 5: 945–75.

Grover, V., R. L. Purvis, and A. H. Segars. 2007. "Exploring Ambidextrous Innovation Tendencies in the Adoption of Telecommunication Technologies." *IEEE Transactions on Engineering Management* 54, no. 2: 268–85.

Gupta, Anil K., Ken G. Smith, and Christina E. Shalley. 2006. "The Interplay between Exploration and Exploitation." *Academy of Management Journal* 49, no. 4 (August): 693–706.

Heavey, Ciaran. 2009. "A Dynamic Managerial Capabilities Model of Organizational Ambidexterity." PhD dissertation, University of Connecticut. ProQuest Dissertations & Theses: A&I (AAT 3401995).

Jansen, Justin J. P., Michiel P. Tempelaar, Frans A. J. van den Bosch, and Henk W. Volberda. 2009. "Structural Differentiation and Ambidexterity: The Mediating Role of Integration Mechanisms." *Organization Science* 20, no. 4: 797–811.

Jantz, Ronald C. 2013. "Incremental and Radical Innovations in Research Libraries: An Exploratory Examination Regarding the Effects of Ambidexterity, Organizational Structure, Leadership, and Contextual Factors" Doctoral dissertation, Rutgers University. doi:10.7282/T3ZP44PT.

Lin, Ming, and Zhu Zhang. 2008. "Question-Driven Segmentation of Lecture Speech Text: Towards Intelligent E-learning Systems." *Journal of the American Society for Information Science and Technology* 59, no. 2 (January): 186–200.

Lubatkin, Michael H., Zeki Simsek, Yan Ling, and John F. Veiga. 2006. "Ambidexterity and Performance in Small- to Medium-Sized Firms: The Pivotal Role of Top Management Team Behavioral Integration." *Journal of Management* 32, no. 5 (October): 646–72.

March, James G. 1991. "Exploration and Exploitation in Organizational Learning." *Organization Science* 2, no. 1: 71–87.

McDonald, Robert H., and Chuck Thomas. 2006. "Disconnects between Library Culture and Millennial Generation Values." *Educause Quarterly* 4 (January 1): 4–6.

O'Reilly III, Charles A., and Michael L. Tushman. 2004. "The Ambidextrous Organization." *Harvard Business Review*, April: 74–81.

———. 2008. "Ambidexterity as a Dynamic Capability: Resolving the Innovator's Dilemma." *Research in Organizational Behavior,* 28: 185–206.

Piao, Ming. 2010. "Thriving in the New: Implication of Exploration on Organizational Longevity." *Journal of Management* 36, no. 6: 1529–54.

Raisch, Sebastian, Julian Birkinshaw, Gilbert Probst, and Michael L. Tushman. 2009. "Organizational Ambidexterity: Balancing Exploitation and Exploration for Sustained Performance." *Organization Science* 20, no. 4: 685–95.

Shane, M. Lanning. 1940. "Audio-visual Aids and the Library." *College and Research Libraries* 1, no. 2 (March): 143–46, 169.

Shepstone, Carol, and Lyn Currie. 2008. "Transforming the Academic Library: Creating an Organizational Culture That Fosters Staff Success." *Journal of Academic Librarianship* 34, no. 4 (July): 358–68.

Shera, Jesse Hauk. 1966. *Documentation and the Organization of Knowledge.* Hamden, CT: Archon Books.

Smith, Wendy K., and Michael L. Tushman. 2005. "Managing Strategic Contradictions: A Top Management Model for Managing Innovation Streams." *Organization Science* 16, no. 5: 522–36.

Tushman, Michael L., and Charles A. O'Reilly III. 1996. "Ambidextrous Organizations: Managing Evolutionary and Revolutionary Change." *California Management Review* 38, no. 4 (Summer): 8–30.

Warner, Rebecca M. 2013. *Applied Statistics: From Bivariate through Multivariate Techniques.* Thousand Oaks, CA: Sage.

Chapter 7

Organizational Structures:
Loose or Tight?

SCHOLARS HAVE USED THE terms *loose* and *tight* to characterize organizations, suggesting that the looser organization has less hierarchy and fewer rules that would restrict innovation. Burns and Stalker (1961, 105) introduced the concepts of mechanistic and organic structures where the organic or loose structure promotes the free flow of ideas and is, presumably, more innovative. Mechanistic structures work best in stable environments, and organic structures are more appropriate in dynamic environments (Damanpour 1991; Damanpour and Gopalakrishnan 1998). The mechanistic structure (figure 7.1a) is more hierarchical with a centralized authority and much of the communication follows the formal structures of the organization. In contrast, the organic structure (figure 7.1b) has a decentralized authority in which communication flows more freely in all directions. In an extensive meta-analysis, Damanpour and Aravind (2012, 493) found that the characteristics associated with the organic structure are more conducive to innovation than those associated with the mechanistic structure.

Organizational Structure—Complexity, Centralization, Formalization

By way of definition, we focus in this study on primary structure that includes the formal structure found in an organization chart—hierarchy, formal processes, supporting units, and job descriptions for organiza-

FIGURE 7.1
Mechanistic and Organic Structures

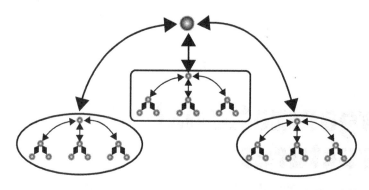

A "Tight" Mechanistic Structure (7.1a)

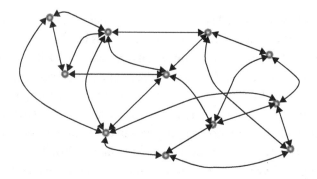

A "Loose" Organic Structure (7.1b)

tional members (Galunic and Eisenhardt 1994, 217–18). Organizational structure is important for innovation insofar as it is designed to facilitate the generation of new ideas and the successful implementation of these ideas. Duncan (1976, 176) has identified the persistent dilemma for innovative organizations: "different organizational structures appear to be appropriate for the initiation and implementation stages of the innovation process." In the initiation stage, a looser organization with less formalism and hierarchy will allow for the generation and free flow of ideas that can become innovations. However, in the implementation stage, more emphasis on process and rules is needed to meet the schedule, quality, and reliability requirements of the new product or service.

Throughout the past several decades of innovation research, scholars have studied various aspects of organizational structure. From this research, three foundational concepts of structure have emerged—complexity, centralization, and formalization (Damanpour and Aravind 2012, 498; Duncan 1976, 173–79; Hage and Aiken 1970, 32–44). Organizational complexity is typically operationalized in terms of functional diversity—the variety and number of different units and the variety of different job specialties. The functional diversity and task specialization brings new knowledge into the organization that can lead to ideas for innovative new services. Most research has shown that complexity is positively related to organizational innovation. In a reexamination of theories regarding structure and innovation, Damanpour and Gopalakrishnan (1998) suggest that organizational complexity in an unstable but predictable environment will result in the initiation of more incremental and radical innovations.

In contrast to complexity, bureaucratic control is generally considered to be negatively associated with innovation. The two major dimensions of bureaucratic control are centralization and formalization. Centralization, or top-down decision making, restricts librarians and staff from access to information and participating in establishing the strategy and priorities of the organization, leading to a lack of commitment by organizational members. In the more hierarchical organization, members will adhere to the formal channels of communication, typically passing along only positive information and neglecting negative feedback that would help the organization improve (Duncan 1976, 177). Formalization refers to a rule-based organization where enforcement of rules restricts creativity and the generation of new ideas. The combination of centralization and formalization results in the bureaucracy's negative impact on innovation, a condition that is cited frequently as a major impediment to large and complex organizations becoming more effective (Tornatzky and Klein 1982).

Based on these perspectives, it would appear that a complex organization with less centralization and formalization is needed in the initiation stage in order to generate and communicate new ideas that are potential innovations. A less complex organization, however, with more adherence to process and top-down decision making is needed in the adoption and implementation stages in order to develop a high-quality, timely, and reliable new service. Leaders seeking a more innovative library are faced with a dilemma in how to create the organizational structure that will facilitate both the initiation and implementation of innovations.

Contingency Theory—Environment and Strategy

What are the conditions that would cause library leaders to change the structure of the organization to become more innovative? Contingency theory proposes that organization effectiveness is dependent on several contextual factors. Two primary structural contingencies are the external environment and the strategy of the organization. Contingency theorists propose that the organization should examine how its structure "fits" with the external environment and organizational strategy. Organizations will strive for a good fit on the premise that this will lead to improved performance (Donaldson 2001, 1–8).

The strategy contingency relates to the unit structure of the organization. A functional structure fits a strategy that focuses on a single product or service and emphasizes efficiency. For most of research library history, the institution focused on primarily one service—the provision of information in the form of books and journals to students and faculty. The very functional and classical organization consisting of public and technical units has served the library mission quite well. As the library moves into providing many different types of services, a more diversified strategy is needed in which units are focused on new services and where each unit has budget accountability and autonomy to make decisions that benefit the specific service. Donaldson (2001, 3) characterizes the strategy-structural dilemma that is faced by research libraries:

> An organization with a diversified strategy that seeks to use the misfitting, functional structure will find top management overwhelmed by the number of decisions and also suffer from lack of responsiveness to markets so that the organization becomes ineffective.

Conversely, an organization with a functional strategy that is attempting to deploy multiple and quite different products and services will focus on efficiency rather than devoting the energy to providing high-quality service for each unique product offering.

Contingency theory also suggests that the structure of the organization and internal functions should adapt to and align with various factors in the external environment in order to survive and prosper (Donaldson 2001, 8–16; Lawrence and Lorsch 1967). Given a stable environment and relatively routine operations, a mechanistic structure and top-down authority works well since managers have sufficient knowledge to make decisions. However, an organization with a mechanistic structure in an unstable environment will not generate the ideas necessary for innovation to flourish. In an organic structure and dynamic environment, knowledge is more distributed among all organizational levels, and decentralized decision making results in more innovation (Donaldson 2001, 2).

The Research Library Organizational Structure

The organizational structure of the library can facilitate or restrict its ability to innovate. Budd (2012, 104–9) has traced the evolution of academic libraries, noting that the bifurcation into public and technical services units was motivated in the early 20th century by a focus on efficient management. To meet the demands for efficiency and cost-effective operation, library managers have created structures with a set of well-defined tasks. The resulting bureaucratic organization creates uniformity based on rules and regulations—management processes that limit creativity and restrict individual discretion. According to Budd, in spite of considerable discussion and espousal of different structures, most research libraries have retained this classical organizational structure that focuses on public services and technical services.

Structure and Innovation in ARL Libraries

The relationship of organizational structure to innovation is strategically important for library leaders and managers. The objective in this study was to examine how the library organizational structure affected the ability to innovate.

In the ARL study, the complexity of the organization was examined by using the concept of structural differentiation—the subdivision of library tasks into different units of the library with an emphasis on separating exploratory and production work (Jansen et al. 2009). Survey respondents indicated their agreement or disagreement to statements such as the following: "In our library, exploratory and production activities are structurally separated."[19] Hypothesis H3 (figure 4.2), which proposed a negative relationship between structural differentiation and innovation performance, was supported in the regression analysis—more differentiation resulted in reduced innovation performance.

Intuitively, one might expect that more structural differentiation would result in different skill sets and new knowledge, culminating in a more innovative library. The explanation for the counterintuitive and negative impact on innovation performance relates to contingency theory and strategy. Donaldson's (2001) observation suggests that a misfit between strategy and structure results in managers being overwhelmed with making decisions in a confusing and inconsistent environment. In effect, the library maintains a functional strategy (public and technical services) while attempting to move into new service offerings that do not fit conveniently into these established structures. These classical structures limit innovation to the specific activities and services that are offered by that unit. In this environment, it would be unusual for librarians to develop new knowledge for totally new services or enhancements to existing services provided by another unit. As a consequence, the more radical, cross-unit ideas and the associated new knowledge are not developed and acted upon, thus reducing innovation performance. This lack of fit between strategy and structure makes it difficult for the library to take advantage of a more differentiated structure to improve innovation performance. Although many research libraries have strategic statements committing to aligning their structures with the changing needs of the university, in practice they still retain the classical structures that were put in place decades ago.

The many factors associated with how structure affects innovation have led to mixed empirical results. The findings, specifically as related to exploratory work and R&D, present a conundrum for library management. In a second wave of meta-analysis, Damanpour and Aravind (2012) found that arguments favoring different structures for initiation and implementation of an innovation require further scrutiny. The research of Moynihan and Landuyt (2009) regarding the learning organization pro-

---

[19] See questions 10 through 14 on the innovation survey (Jantz 2013).

vides insight into this dilemma. In an empirical study of a public service organization, these researchers have found that both culture and structure are intertwined and mutually dependent. Whereas the development of a learning culture will take time, the use of formal structural mechanisms can have a more immediate effect on organizational learning.

New Structures for the Library

A way forward for the research library would include an alignment between strategy and structure in order to become more innovative and provide the support for new services. Possibilities include specific structures for R&D and new service offerings.

Exploratory Work

Establishing an R&D unit in the library will require a more concerted effort directed at how exploratory efforts are managed and strategically integrated into the traditional structures of the library. Managing R&D requires the library leader to address projects that are characterized by a high degree of uncertainty, intensity, and autonomy. These projects with less well-defined schedules and unfamiliar vocabulary will be carried out in parallel with mainstream projects. Research suggests that R&D teams or units, buffered from those units supporting current services and with a high degree of autonomy, are necessary for innovation and high performance (Payne 1990, 118). In a study of knowledge-intensive business services, Amara, Landry, and Doloreux (2009) found that R&D had a positive impact on all six forms of innovation, including process, management, and strategic innovation.

R&D units can benefit the library in several ways. First, creative ideas that impact the whole library are more likely to emanate from a unit that is not located within one of the traditional units that support existing technical or public services. Secondly, although members of a new R&D unit might be doing original research, one of the primary tasks within the library is to boundary span, transfer technology from other domains (commercial and nonprofit), and explore how this technology can be adapted for use. The objective is not only to take advantage of these new technologies but also to accelerate the transfer of technology into the library for the benefit of users within the university. Dedicated R&D budgets, portfolio management, flexibility, and a view of long-term benefits will all be needed in order to reap the benefits of this more focused research (Daellenbach, McCarthy, and Schoenecker 1999; Mikkola 2001; Thambain 2003).

The Structure for New Services

To face the library future, Jim Neal states, "We should participate in the entrepreneurial academy by leveraging assets to advance new markets and new products and by building a culture of competition, risk, and innovation" (quoted in Alire and Evans 2010, 345). Although the traditional public services and technical services units have served the research library well, these structures were not meant to be permanent and will not work well for the new markets that Neal proposes. In 1984, Patricia Battin (172) stated that the new communication technologies demand radically different organizational structures in order to support new integrated services. Budd (2012, 109) reports on the library's continued dependence on these traditional structures and the resistance to change, in part due to the tension between organizing for efficiency versus total organizational effectiveness. Budd asserts, "Reorganization based on effectiveness may well lead the library away from the bureaucratic model." Budd's statement is profound and compelling, suggesting a totally different view of the research library and one that should cause leaders to rethink their definition of effectiveness, performance, and structure.

In this era of rapid change and new opportunities, the traditional library units restrict the ability to focus on a specific service and to act quickly. Individual members within these units find it difficult and confusing to understand library-wide priorities that are frequently established by obscure processes and management mandates. The creation of units or teams that are focused on a specific service with a high degree of autonomy and budget authority clarifies priorities and enables fast action in developing the service and responding to users. Examples of services that might be offered by these units include support for science data, scholarly publishing (e-journals, e-textbooks, ETDs), digital humanities, and institutional repositories.

All of these important new services could be established in separate units. Given the pace of change in the information environment, an effective strategy will create and disband these special units as necessary. As one example of more rapid restructuring that is possible, the University of Illinois Library in the period 2008–2011 designed *and* implemented approximately 20 major reorganization initiatives (Conner 2014, 136). Although research libraries are addressing more innovative structures, many of the new service ventures remain embedded in the traditional units or spread across multiple units.

Conclusion

The empirical results of the ARL study demonstrate that structure can affect the innovation performance of the library. Although there are emerging library structures that show promise, it is likely that the classical structure of the library will need to be significantly altered in order to support an innovative culture. In identifying some of the classic innovation traps, Kanter (2013, 121–22) suggests loosening formal controls and tightening human connections between exploratory teams and those supporting existing services are important actions. Kanter also states that a major process mistake is "strangling of innovation with tight planning, budgeting, and reviews," actions that are useful for existing products and services but can stifle the more entrepreneurial spirit (104).

Organizational structure can be used strategically to become more innovative, supporting R&D with diverse skills and competencies. Strong performance management systems, coupled with these structural conditions, will lead to more successful innovations (Damanpour and Aravind 2012, 509). The critical issues for library management are the alignment of a diversified strategy with revised organizational structures and providing the connectivity and communication to integrate these more diverse units. Yet it is important to recognize that any structure is contingent, not permanent, and will have to be changed frequently in order to adapt to a dynamic environment and an evolving strategy.

References

Alire, Camilla A., and G. Edward Evans. 2010. *Academic Librarianship.* New York: Neal-Schuman.

Amara, Nabil, Réjean Landry, and David Doloreux. 2009. "Patterns of Innovation in Knowledge-Intensive Business Services." *Services Industries Journal* 29, no. 4: 407–30.

Battin, Patricia. 1984. "The Library: Center of the Restructured University." *College and Research Libraries* 45, no. 3 (May): 170–76. doi:10.5860/crl_45_03_170.

Budd, John M. 2012. *The Changing Academic Library: Operations, Culture, Environments.* Chicago: Association of College and Research Libraries.

Burns, Tom, and G. M. Stalker. 1961. *The Management of Innovation.* London: Tavistock.

Conner, Matthew. 2014. *The New University Library: Four Case Studies.* Chicago: American Library Association.

Daellenbach, Urs S., Anne M. McCarthy, and Timothy S. Schoenecker. 1999. "Commitment to Innovation: The Impact of Top Management Team Characteristics." *R&D Management* 29, no. 3 (July): 199–208.

Damanpour, Fariborz. 1991. "Organizational Innovation: A Meta-analysis of Effects of Determinants and Moderators." *Academy of Management Journal* 34, no. 3 (September): 555–90.

Damanpour, Fariborz, and Deepa Aravind. 2012. "Organizational Structure and Innovation Revisited: From Organic to Ambidextrous Structure." In *Handbook of Organizational Creativity*, edited by Michael D. Mumford, 483–513. Waltham, MA: Academic Press.

Damanpour, Fariborz, and Shanthi Gopalakrishnan. 1998. "Theories of Organizational Structure and Innovation Adoption: The Role of Environmental Change." *Journal of Engineering and Technology Management* 15, no. 1 (March): 1–24.

Donaldson, Lex. 2001. *The Contingency Theory of Organizations.* Thousand Oaks, CA: Sage Publications.

Duncan, R. B. 1976. "The Ambidextrous Organization: Designing Dual Structures for Innovation." In *The Management of Organization Design: Strategies and Implementation*, edited by Ralph H. Killman, Louis R. Pondy, and Dennis P. Slevin, 167–88. New York: North-Holland.

Galunic, D. C., and K. M. Eisenhardt. 1994. "Renewing the Strategy-Structure-Performance Paradigm." In *Research in Organizational Behavior*, vol. 16, edited by Barry M. Staw and Larry L. Cummings, 215–55. Greenwich, CT: JAI Press.

Hage, Jerald, and Michael Aiken. 1970. *Social Change in Complex Organizations.* New York: Random House.

Jansen, Justin J. P., Michiel P. Tempelaar, Frans A. J. van den Bosch, and Henk W. Volberda. 2009. "Structural Differentiation and Ambidexterity: The Mediating Role of Integration Mechanisms." *Organization Science* 20, no. 4: 797–811.

Jantz, Ronald C. 2013. "Incremental and Radical Innovations—Survey," May 20, doi:10.7282/T37D2S88.

Kanter, Rosabeth Moss. 2013. "Innovation: The Classic Traps." In *HBR's 10 Must Reads on Innovation*, 101–24. Boston: Harvard Business Review Press.

Lawrence, Paul R., and Jay W. Lorsch. 1967. "Differentiation and Integration in Complex Organizations." *Administrative Science Quarterly* 12, no. 1 (June): 1–47.

Mikkola, Juliana Hsuan. 2001. "Portfolio Management of R&D Projects: Implications for Innovation Management." *Technovation* 21, no. 7 (July): 423–35.

Moynihan, Donald P., and Noel Landuyt. 2009. "How Do Public Organizations Learn? Bridging Cultural and Structural Perspectives." *Public Administration Review* 69, no. 6 (November/December): 1097–105.

Payne, Roy. 1990. "The Effectiveness of Research Team: A Review." In *Innovation and Creativity at Work: Psychological and Organizational Strategies*, edited by Michael A. West and James L. Farr, 101–22. New York: John Wiley & Sons.

Thambain, Hans J. 2003. "Managing Innovative R&D Teams." *R&D Management* 33, no. 3 (June): 297–311.

Tornatzky, Louis G., and Katherine J. Klein. 1982. "Innovation Characteristics and Innovation Adoption-Implementation: A Meta-analysis of Findings." *IEEE Transactions on Engineering Management* 29, no. 1 (February): 28–43.

Chapter 8

Trigger Events and Jolts from the External Environment

SOME 25 YEARS AGO, Herbert White[20] (1990, 54) speculated on what lies ahead for the library in the 21st century. In looking inward, White states, "We are unable to assess factors outside of our own discipline." White raises an intriguing question regarding the ability of professional librarians to examine and respond to the external environment in ways that will benefit the institution. In commenting on the growth of libraries, Shera (1971, 30) emphasizes the importance of responding to changes in the environment:

> The great danger to libraries lies not in their growth *per se*, but in the possibility of their failure to adapt intellectually to a changing environment, as the prehistoric creatures were unable to adjust physically when the Mesozoic gave way to the Cenozoic.

The research library as an institutional nonprofit is embedded in an environment that can be especially resistant to innovation. Bass (1985, 160) has noted that changes are particularly difficult to effect in the public university, and Duderstadt (2000, 37) writes that the university responds to external forces by defending the status quo, resulting in change at a glacial pace within traditional paradigms. In his study of the resistance to

---

[20] In 1990, Herbert S. White was dean and professor at the School of Library and Information Science, Indiana University, Bloomington.

innovation in higher education, Evans (1970, 4) notes that the university community "has been successful in resisting change, even though a dynamic and far more complex society has evolved around it."

The External Environment

The research literature has been quite consistent in suggesting that innovation is stimulated by events in the external environment (Bierly and Daly 2007; Freel 2005; Jun and Weare 2011; Light 1998, 13–16; Russell and Russell 1992). Although there is considerable literature on innovation and public institutions, Noordegraaf and Stewart (2000) suggest that more attention should be given to the environment in which the institution is embedded. During difficult and turbulent times, created possibly by technological advances or changing economic circumstances, an organization becomes more vulnerable to the influences from external forces. For much of the 20th century, research libraries resided in a stable, predictable environment, focusing primarily on incremental innovations that improved efficiency and quality of service. However, the external environment of the 21st-century research library appears to be much more dynamic, a situation that can lead to organic and less bureaucratic organizations that are more conducive to major innovations.

Outside of the borders of the university, there are external pressures that are creating environmental uncertainty that can impact the university and the research library. These external pressures originate, in part, from the political and economic environment and the emergence of for-profit firms that offer competing library services. Educational institutions such as Phoenix University and Kaplan University are favorites on Wall Street and are among for-profit providers that have profit margins of up to 19.4 percent (Meisenhelder 2013). Although these firms are spending more on advertising and recruitment than on instruction, they represent attractive alternatives to students who are looking for a low-cost education.

The economic environment is also a source of considerable uncertainty and apprehension in many universities. Harvard University officials have warned of "rapid, disorienting change" at colleges and universities, citing the difficulty of meeting the aspirations of the institution within current budget constraints (Martin 2012). Recently, events in the state of Wisconsin, driven in part by budget deficits, are creating concerns on the

University of Wisconsin campus. A state legislative committee approved proposals that would eliminate the faculty's role in shared governance and also eliminate laws that protect tenure (Kelderman 2015).

In a nonprofit organization, managers have little or no direct control in determining the amount of financial resources to be allocated to the organization. The declining budget of the research library remains a major challenge for institutional leaders. Budd (1998, 196–98) cites a trend that started in the mid-1970s in which the academic library's expenditures began to shrink as a part of the parent institution's educational and general expenditures. The data on 1,000 four-year institutions show a decline in this percentage in a decade (1976–1985) from 5.05 percent to 3.73 percent. The budgets of 88 ARL libraries fell steadily in a decade (1982–1992) from 3.91 percent to 3.32 percent of the university's education and general budget (Allen and Dickie 2007). Figure 8.1 dramatically illustrates this continuing trend, showing a decline of library expenditures from 3.7 percent to 1.8 percent of university expenditures for 40 research libraries during the period 1982 to 2011 (ARL 2013).

FIGURE 8.1
The Decline of ARL Library Expenditures

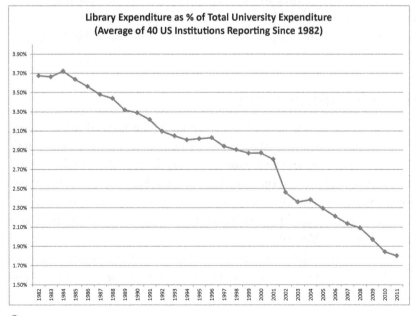

Obviously, the library has done a great job at becoming more efficient and managing costs. Consolidation of physical spaces and discontinuing print journal subscriptions are two examples. Still, leaders can hardly ignore the not-so-subtle budget message that the library is no longer meeting the needs of the university and financial resources are being systematically redirected to other units in the institution.

Beyond the competitive threats and financial constraints, rapidly evolving technology is resulting in major, disruptive events for the university. Technology advances are a major factor and a key to understanding how environments and organizations evolve over time (Tushman and Anderson 1986). A high-technology environment is quite different from a low-technology environment, resulting in more uncertainty and more complexity. What appears to be virtually unlimited growth in computing storage capacity, processing power, and network bandwidth augurs convincingly for an era of revolutionary technology impacting the research library. Research and prototypes are emerging routinely outside the library. For example, an intelligent robotic books-retrieval system utilizing RFID tags opens the possibility of fewer staff required in the library (Yuan et al. 2002). Neural networks are yielding remarkable progress in image classification and speech recognition, applications that could significantly enhance library multimedia collections (Anthes 2013). Artificial intelligence and adaptive learning techniques can be used to significantly improve reference services and bibliographic instruction.

Trigger Events and Jolts

During difficult times, created possibly by technological advances or changing economic circumstances, an organization becomes more vulnerable to the influences from external forces. The members of the library, including the leaders, will typically follow their daily routines until there is some external event that forces a change. In the innovation literature, these events are referred to as jolts, trigger events, or shocks (Bierly and Daly 2007; Van de Ven 1986).

The innovation diffusion process of figure 3.1 highlights the importance of a variety of enablers, including trigger events in the external environment, which can stimulate innovative thinking in the organization. These jolts in the for-profit sector include performance indicators such as profit/loss and return-on-investment reports, focusing leadership on the necessity for change. In addition to these more objective indicators, the emergence of a strong competitor can cause a business leader to take action. In the research library, competition is much more muted, and quantitative performance indicators are not available, resulting in the lack of any compelling reason to initiate a major change. For the library, trigger events might include technology advancements, a peer library's success with a major innovation, and demands from the parent institution or state politicians to become more efficient and reduce expenditures. Perhaps the most obvious external jolt in today's research library is the continued downward pressure on the budget, impacting the library's ability to purchase books and journals and create promising new services.

Measuring Uncertainty and Dynamism in the External Environment

Does the research library reside in a dynamic and uncertain environment? Boyne and Meier (2009) clarify the concept of environmental dynamism by explaining that the crucial element is not the frequency or magnitude of change, which can usually be anticipated, but the unpredictability or uncertainty of the environment. As noted previously, the environment does not create change directly; rather, it is the perceptions of the environment by key actors and the related initiatives that result in organizational change. It is possible that a leader may not perceive a complex external environment as turbulent, resulting in the leader not taking action to respond to external stimuli.

For the statistical analysis in this study and in accordance with Milliken (1987) and Waldman and colleagues (2001), *environmental uncertainty* was constructed as a perception by leaders of conditions external to the university library. A six-item scale, adapted from Khandwalla (1976) and Koberg and Ungson (1987), was used to measure environmental uncertainty as perceived by library leaders.

Library Leaders' Perceptions of the Environment

In the study of innovation in ARL libraries, library leaders' responses were combined to create a single factor representing each organization's view of environmental uncertainty. Perceptions of a benign environment may induce complacency and a commitment to the status quo, attitudes that work against innovation (Hambrick 1994, 193). In the ARL study, the research hypothesis (H4 in figure 4.2) was stated as follows: "Uncertainty in the external environment, as perceived by library leaders, is positively related to innovation performance in the research library." It was expected that more uncertainty would lead to improved innovation performance because leaders would take action to address external conditions that might affect the library. Hypothesis H4 was not supported in the regression analysis. Of the major factors in the research model, the external environment was the only factor that was not significantly related to innovation performance.

In a further analysis, four questions were used from the six-item scale that uniquely captures the respondent's ability to predict various aspects of the library environment. These questions probe the leaders' ability to predict change in four areas: funding for the library, government regulatory control, political attitude toward the library, and the actions of peer institutions. A sample survey statement requiring a response on a nine-point Likert scale was the following: "I can accurately predict the impact of the political attitude of the community and other public constituencies toward the university and the library."[21] For each item, a leadership team score was computed as an average of the scores for each individual team member. The scores were reversed to represent *unpredictability* on these dimensions. To develop an organizational score that represents the team's perception of the unpredictability of the external environment, the mean team scores for each scale item were averaged, resulting in a final score for the research library. The unpredictability mean for all library teams was 3.71 on a nine-point Likert scale (SD = 0.75, N = 50). The team scores for each of the leadership teams in the 50 ARL research libraries are depicted in figure 8.2. The y-axis represents the unique identifier for each library, and the x-axis is the unpredictability score for each library.

---

[21] See questions 15–20 on the innovation survey (Jantz 2013).

FIGURE 8.2
Research Library Team Perceptions of the External Environment (*N* = 50)

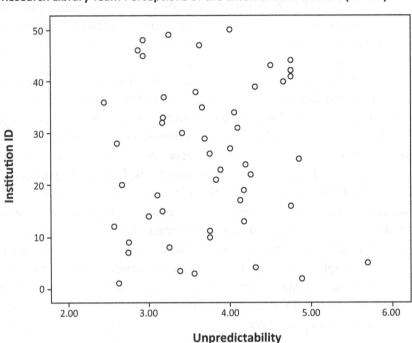

It is evident from the scatter plot of figure 8.2, where all scores except one are less than 5.0 and many hover between 2.5 and 3.5, that most of the library leadership teams were reasonably confident that they could predict events in the external environment that might affect the library.

Although the leadership teams' views of the external environment did not have a significant impact on innovative performance in the research library, it is instructive to examine the data more closely. By using the mean to dichotomize unpredictability and *innovation performance*, all 50 libraries are placed in one of four quadrants as in table 8.1.

TABLE 8.1
Predictability versus Innovative Performance for ARL Libraries (*N* = 50)

	Innovative	Not Innovative
Unpredictable	13	12
Predictable	14	11

As see in the table, 13 research libraries whose leadership teams viewed the environment as unpredictable were innovative, as compared to 14 libraries that were innovative and perceived the external environment to be predictable. Given the almost uniform distribution across the four quadrants of table 8.1, the unpredictability factor did not have a significant impact on innovation performance.

The theoretical perspective and numerous empirical studies (Baldridge and Burnham 1975; Damanpour 1996; Davis 2003; Koberg and Ungson 1987; Koberg, Detienne, and Heppard 2003) suggest organizations that exist in a dynamic environment will respond by initiating innovative approaches to address the risk posed by the more uncertain environment. In his study of small business firms, Freel (2005) notes specifically that perceived higher levels of human resource uncertainty and difficulty in recruiting required skill sets in service organizations are associated with increased innovation. However, the theoretical approach, as evidenced in these studies, did not hold for the 50 ARL libraries in the study sample. In an opposing theoretical perspective, researchers have suggested that managers might respond more conservatively to environmental turbulence. In studying public organizations, Andrews (2009) hypothesized that managers in a turbulent environment might become increasingly cautious and less willing to develop new services. This hypothesis was supported with both objective and subjective measures of environmental turbulence. In a study of Texas school districts, Boyne and Meier (2009) found that environmental turbulence had a negative impact on organizational performance, suggesting that managers mitigate the harmful effects of a volatile environment by maintaining structural stability.

Both theory and methods are implicated in the mixed results regarding innovation and the perceptions of the external environment. It is important to acknowledge the long-standing methodological challenge in capturing *environmental uncertainty* as a variable in an empirical analysis. Researchers have cited substantial differences in the use of objective and subjective measures to assess various aspects of the environment (Boyne and Meier 2009; Kuivalainen et al. 2004; Milliken 1987). Perceptions are an important variable in empirical analyses. However, they may suffer from respondent bias. Obviously, some library managers will overstate the degree of uncertainty while others might view the environment as relatively benign. In this study, variance in leader response was mitigated by averaging the views of the entire leadership team to create the perception of environmental uncertainty for the library.

For objective measures, researchers have used population density and ethnic diversity as proxies for environmental complexity. Andrews (2009) found, however, that both objective and subjective measures of the environment were similarly related to organizational performance. There is little convincing research that either contradicts or supports the generally accepted belief that top administrators can provide reliable information about their organizations (Koberg et al. 2003). Although self-assessment measures can be prone to bias, they are the most commonly used approach, given that other measures are difficult to obtain and can also be biased (Gatignon et al. 2002).

Conclusion

Organizational scholars have pointed out that one of the most lethal aspects of a turbulent environment is the inability of leaders to predict the impact on their organization (Anderson and Tushman 2001; Boyne and Meier 2009). What we see in the ARL analysis is a group of library leaders who are confident that they understand external pressures and who are familiar with what their peer institutions are doing. However, it is possible that leaders with long tenure in the profession may not be undertaking the boundary spanning and external communication that is required to properly assess the potential impact of a dynamic environment.

The predominant theoretical argument holds that environmental dynamism will result in more organizational innovation in order to cope with the uncertainty. As Hurley and Hult (1998) suggest, adaptation to a rapidly changing external environment will require the adoption of new behaviors and the creation of a greater capacity to innovate. This argument probably fits best with the for-profit sector and organizations that are seeking a competitive edge. In fact, for a nonprofit institution like the library, we might expect less innovation in turbulent times where leaders choose to stabilize their organizations rather than take on more risk. We are left with the possibilities that library leaders are aware of the more dynamic environment and have consciously chosen not to address the uncertainty or, alternatively, they are so embedded in the norms and traditions of the profession that it becomes very difficult to step outside of these boundaries.

A vibrant, capitalist economy will continue to encroach on the domain that has traditionally been the uncontested market of the research library. University administrators will ask the library to do more with less. However, the library is not a passive victim of these forces in the external environment; opportunities are plentiful in collaboration with external agents, the transfer of technology for adaptation to library services, and the tapping of a rich source of new ideas and knowledge.

References

Allen, Frank R., and Mark Dickie. 2007. "Toward a Formula-Based Model for Academic Library Funding: Statistical Significance and Implications of a Model Based upon Institutional Characteristics." *College and Research Libraries* 68, no. 2 (March): 170–81.

Anderson, Philip, and Michael L. Tushman. 2001. "Organizational Environments and Industry Exit: The Effects of Uncertainty, Munificence and Complexity." *Industrial and Corporate Change* 10, no. 3: 675–711.

Andrews, Rhys. 2009. "Organizational Task Environments and Performance: An Empirical Analysis." *International Public Management Journal* 12, no. 1: 1–23.

Anthes, Gary. 2013. "Deep Learning Comes of Age." *Communications of the ACM* 56, no. 6: 13–15.

ARL (Association of Research Libraries). 2013. "Library Expenditure as % of Total University Expenditure (Average of 40 US Institutions Reporting Since 1982)." http://www.libqual.org/documents/admin/EG_2.pdf.

Baldridge, J. Victor, and Robert A. Burnham. 1975. "Organizational Innovation: Individual, Organizational, and Environmental Impacts." *Administrative Science Quarterly* 20, no. 2 (June): 165–76.

Bass, Bernard M. 1985. *Leadership and Performance beyond Expectations.* New York: Free Press.

Bierly III, Paul E., and Paula S. Daly. 2007. "Alternative Knowledge Strategies, Competitive Environment, and Organizational Performance in Small Manufacturing Firms." *Entrepreneurship Theory and Practice* 31, no. 4 (July): 493–516.

Boyne, George A., and Kenneth J. Meier. 2009. "Environmental Turbulence, Organizational Stability, and Public Service Performance." *Administration and Society* 40, no. 8 (January): 799–824.

Budd, John M. 1998. *The Academic Library: Its Context, Its Purpose, and Its Operation.* Englewood, CO: Libraries Unlimited.

Damanpour, Fariborz. 1996. "Organizational Complexity and Innovation: Developing and Testing Multiple Contingency Models." *Management Science* 42, no. 5
(May): 693–716.

Davis, Carolyn D. 2003. "Organizational Innovation: The Role of Top Management in
Different Stages of Innovation Implementation." PhD dissertation, Georgia Institute of Technology. ProQuest Dissertations & Theses: A&I (AAT 3110401).

Duderstadt, James J. 2000. *A University for the 21st Century.* Ann Arbor: University of
Michigan Press.

Evans, Richard I. 1970. *Resistance to Innovation in Higher Education.* San Francisco:
Jossey-Bass.

Freel, Mark S. 2005. "Perceived Environmental Uncertainty and Innovation in Small
Firms." *Small Business Economics* 25, no. 1 (August): 49–64.

Gatignon, Hubert, Michael L. Tushman, Wendy Smith, and Philip Anderson. 2002.
"A Structural Approach to Assessing Innovation: Construct Development of
Innovation Locus, Type, and Characteristics." *Management Science* 48, no. 9:
1103–22.

Hambrick, Donald C. 1994. "Top Management Groups: A Conceptual Integration and
Reconsideration of the 'Team' Label." In *Research in Organizational Behavior,*
vol. 16, edited by Barry M. Staw and Larry L. Cummings, 171–213. Greenwich,
CT: JAI Press.

Hurley, Robert F., and Tomas M. Hult. 1998. "Innovation, Market Orientation, and
Organizational Learning: An Integration and Empirical Examination." *Journal of
Marketing* 62, no. 3 (July): 42–54.

Jantz, Ronald C. 2013. "Incremental and Radical Innovations—Survey," May 20,
doi:10.7282/T37D2S88.

Jun, Kyu-Nahm, and Christopher Weare. 2011. "Institutional Motivations in the Adoption of Innovations: The Case of E-government." *Journal of Public Administration
Research and Theory* 21: 495–519.

Kelderman, Eric. 2015. "Wisconsin Lawmakers Take Aim at Tenure and Shared Governance." *Chronicle of Higher Education,* May 31. http://chronicle.com/article/
Wisconsin-Lawmakers-Take-Aim/230545.

Khandwalla, Pradip N. 1976. *The Design of Organizations.* New York: Harcourt Brace
Jovanovich.

Koberg, Christine S., Dawn R. Detienne, and Kurt A. Heppard. 2003. "An Empirical
Test of Environmental, Organizational, and Process Factors Affecting Incremental and Radical Innovation." *Journal of High Technology Management Research* 14,
no. 1 (Spring): 21–45.

Koberg, Christine S., and Gerardo R. Ungson. 1987. "The Effects of Environmental
Uncertainty and Dependence on Organizational Structure and Performance: A
Comparative Study." *Journal of Management* 13, no. 4 (Winter): 725–37.

Kuivalainen, Olli, Sanna Sundqvist, Kaisu Puumalainen, and John W. Cadogan. 2004. "The Effect of Environmental Turbulence and Leader Characteristics on International Performance: Are Knowledge-Based Firms Different?" *Canadian Journal of Administrative Sciences* 21, no. 1 (March): 35–50.

Light, Paul C. 1998. *Sustaining Innovation: Creating Nonprofit and Government Organizations That Innovate Naturally.* San Francisco: Jossey-Bass.

Martin, Andrew. 2012. "Building a Showcase Campus, Using an I.O.U." *New York Times,* December 13, A1, B4.

Meisenhelder, Susan. 2013. "Investors and Corporations Want to Make Big Profits off MOOCs." *On Campus* 33, no. 2 (Winter): 7–8.

Milliken, Frances J. 1987. "Three Types of Perceived Uncertainty about the Environment: State, Effect and Response Uncertainty." *Academy of Management Review* 12, no. 1 (January): 133–43.

Noordegraaf, Mirko, and Rosemary Stewart. 2000. "Managerial Behavior Research in Private and Public Sectors: Distinctiveness, Disputes and Directions." *Journal of Management Studies* 37, no. 3 (May): 427–43.

Russell, Robert D., and Craig J. Russell. 1992. "An Examination of the Effects of Organizational Norms, Organizational Structure, and Environmental Uncertainty on Entrepreneurial Strategy." *Journal of Management* 18, no. 4: 639–57.

Shera, Jesse Hauk. 1971. *"The Compleat Librarian" and Other Essays.* Cleveland, OH: The Press of Case Western Reserve University.

Tushman, Michael L., and Philip Anderson. 1986. "Technological Discontinuities and Organizational Environments." *Administrative Science Quarterly* 31, no. 3 (September): 439–65.

Van de Ven, Andrew H. 1986. "Central Problems in the Management of Innovation." *Management Science* 32, no. 5 (May): 590–607.

Waldman, David A., Gabriel G. Ramirez, Robert J. House, and Phanish Puranam. 2001. "Does Leadership Matter? CEO Leadership Attributes and Profitability under Conditions of Perceived Environmental Uncertainty." *Academy of Management Journal* 44, no. 1 (February): 134–43.

White, Herbert S. 1990. "Libraries and Librarians in the Next Millennium. *Library Journal* 115, no. 9 (May 15): 54–55.

Yuan, Kho Hao, Ang Chip Hong, M. Ang, and Goi Sio Peng. 2002. "Unmanned Library: An Intelligent Robotic Books Retrieval and Return System Utilizing RFID Tags." In *Systems, Man and Cybernetics, 2002 IEEE International Conference,* vol. 4. doi:10.1109/ICSMC.2002.1173317.

Chapter 9

Unexpected Results:
The Demographics of the Leadership Team

MUCH OF THE RESEARCH on innovation suggests that organizations led by older teams will be less innovative whereas those led by more educated teams will be more innovative. Wilder (1999, 1) notes that librarians, particularly academic librarians, are older than other professionals in all but a few occupations. For the profession, about 75 percent of librarians are 45 years or older, and the trend appears to be in the direction of increasing age with significant aging occurring after 1990. Tenure in the profession has similar characteristics. Library leaders generally have significant library experience, having spent most of their careers in a library.

Upper echelons theory provides a framework for understanding how the demographics of the leadership team can affect the innovativeness of the research library. In constructing the research model, it was expected that the effects of age and educational level would affect leadership actions in attempting to introduce major change in the library. However, the statistical results were most unexpected—the age and educational level of the library leadership team did not have a significant impact on the innovativeness of the research library.

Upper Echelons Theory and Demographics

Upper echelons theory is premised on the concept of bounded rationali-ty—the idea that leaders, and most everyone else, cannot readily under-stand a complex information environment (Hambrick 2007). Therefore, according to Hambrick, we must consider how the biases, emotions, and dispositions of top executives affect organizational performance. Ham-brick and Mason (1984) developed a model of how these upper echelon characteristics are reflected in organizational outcomes, suggesting that managerial characteristics will partially predict how well the organization performs. They argue that complex decisions, such as those involving the strategy of the organization, are difficult to make based solely on technical and economic factors. For these more complex decisions, leaders are in-clined to make decisions based on behavioral factors. Given the difficulty of obtaining data about behavior and internal cognitive states, researchers can reliably use information about functional backgrounds and tenure to understand leaders' strategic actions (Hambrick 1994, 2007). Based on this theoretical perspective, the ARL study used library leadership age, tenure, and educational level to assess the impact of these characteristics on innovativeness.

The Impact of Leadership Demographics

Many researchers have explored how leadership demographics such as age and tenure can affect organizational performance and the ability to innovate. Several studies have shown that older leadership results in risk-averse behavior that is not likely to lead to innovative practices (Bantel and Jackson 1989; Fernández-Mesa, Iborra, and Safón 2013; Finkelstein and Hambrick 1990; Hambrick 1994, 185). Although there is some vari-ability, the general trends suggest that higher age and longer tenure will adversely affect the organization's ability to innovate. On the other hand, higher educational levels and a more diverse education within the leader-ship team have shown positive correlations with innovativeness.

Bantel and Jackson (1989) examined the characteristics of top man-agement teams (TMTs) in banks including average age, average tenure[22]

---

[22] The focus here is on *organizational tenure*, the number of years a team member has with the specific organization. A related concept is *team tenure*—the number of years one has been a member of a specific team.

in the firm, education level, and heterogeneity with respect to age, tenure, educational background, and functional background. Results indicated that innovative banks are managed by more educated teams who are diverse with respect to their functional areas of expertise. These relationships remained significant when controlling for organizational size and team size. In their study of innovation and education levels in high schools, Daft and Becker (1978, 53) found that teacher professionalism as measured by the percentage of teachers with a master's degree was highly correlated with innovation. In circumstances similar to what might be found in a research library, Davis (2003) studied the phenomenon of implementing technological innovation by focusing on innovations that are purchased in contrast to innovations that are developed in-house. In this study of 241 drug and alcohol treatment centers, she found that education was positively related to the awareness stage of innovation.

Finkelstein and Hambrick (1990) studied executive-team tenure in a sample of 100 organizations in the computer, chemical, and natural gas distribution industries. These researchers found that tenure has a significant impact on strategy and performance, with long-tenured managerial teams following more persistent strategies that conformed to the norms in the industry. Wiersema and Bantel (1992) report firms that are most likely to undergo strategic corporate change had top teams characterized by lower average age, shorter organizational tenure, and higher educational level. Daellenbach, McCarthy, and Schoenecker (1999) report studies of the opposite effects in which years of experience in the industry are positively related to innovation. Using an upper echelons theoretical framework, Carmelo-Ordaz, Hernández-Lara, and Valle-Cabrera (2005) found that TMT tenure has a negative influence on innovation whereas educational level has a positive effect. Damanpour and Schneider (2009) used survey data on 25 innovations in 725 local governments to assess how manager characteristics influence innovation adoption decisions. These researchers report that the age of managers in public organizations was not significantly related to innovation.

In a large empirical study of three industries (aerospace, electronics, and telecommunications), Koberg, Detienne, and Heppard (2003) used complexity theory as a theoretical framework and found that CEO age was negatively associated with incremental innovation (i.e., higher age, less incremental innovation), a result that was contrary to their hypothesis. The effect might be explained by their research protocol that aggregated both administrative innovations (rules, work procedures, work schedules, etc.) and technical innovations together.[23] The Koberg study also reported partial support for CEO age being negatively related to radical innovation. Especially relevant for institutional nonprofits and the research library, these researchers note that managerial variables such as tenure in position and tenure with the company were significant predictors of incremental innovation. Managers who have a long tenure and history with an organization have invested considerable effort in existing services and are more psychologically attuned to preserving the status quo and continuing on an incremental innovation track.

The dispersion or heterogeneity of certain characteristics within the top management team (Bantel and Jackson 1989; Hambrick 1994) can also affect innovation capability. Wiersema and Bantel (1992) note that higher organizational tenure heterogeneity and higher educational specialization heterogeneity are positively related to strategic change. It should be noted that this demographic diversity, however, can be positive only up to a point. At very high levels of diversity, conflict and power struggles are likely to occur.

Table 9.1 provides insight into team age and tenure variation in the 50 libraries in the ARL study, where the standard deviations suggest relatively little diversity in these two factors.

TABLE 9.1
Demographics of the ARL Library Leadership Teams (N = 50)

Variable	Mean	Standard Deviation
Leadership Team Average Age (Years)	55.5	4.13
Leadership Team Average Tenure in the Profession (Years)	25.1	6.15

---

[23] From a methodological perspective, it is best to examine administrative and technical innovations separately since these innovations originate in quite different circumstances (Damanpour and Aravind 2011).

Demographics in ARL Libraries

Although the reported studies of for-profit firms cannot be generalized to research libraries, the aging library profession and long tenure in the position may have significant impact on library innovation performance. It must also be acknowledged that leaders can be flexible, regardless of age, and are able to adjust their management styles based on the specific situation. Indeed, the analysis of library leadership demographics yielded the most unexpected results of the entire study.

Leadership Age and Tenure

Although there are some mixed results, the trends from earlier research suggest that the age of the leadership team will negatively affect innovation while educational levels will positively affect innovation. The ARL library innovation study hypothesized that the leadership average age and tenure in the profession would be negatively associated with innovation performance.

However, the library leadership average age and tenure in profession were not significantly correlated with innovation performance (appendix C). Examination of the scatter plot indicates that an inverted U-shaped distribution for these variables was also not present, suggesting that the middle ranges for age and tenure were also not correlated with innovation performance. To explore these relationships further, leadership team age and innovation performance were dichotomized using the means to create the four quadrants as shown in table 9.2.

As is evident in table 9.2, there is almost a uniform distribution across the four quadrants with the highest frequency in the Young Team—Innovative category. In framing the hypotheses in the library study, it was suggested that younger teams would not have the experience or confidence to support innovation in libraries. Because of career and retirement con-

TABLE 9.2
Distribution of Innovative Libraries and Leadership Team Age ($N = 50$)

	Innovative Libraries	Non-innovative Libraries	Total
Young Teams	15	11	26
Mature Teams	12	12	24
Total	27	23	50

cerns, older teams would be less likely to take on the risk that is associated with major change. In the ARL sample, libraries with younger teams and more mature teams have clearly been able to innovate. These results suggest that other factors are compensating for the possible negative effects of age within the leadership team.

In an alternative perspective, libraries may be achieving more innovative capability from leadership teams that have worked together for prolonged periods. In particular, as discussed in the framing of the mediation hypothesis in chapter six, organizational ambidexterity will take time to develop as the team experiences more positive interactions. Although the exploration of these various causal effects was beyond the scope of the library study, it might be expected that the age of the leadership team would positively affect ambidexterity that in turn has a positive impact on innovation performance. Therefore, the more mature teams may be more ambidextrous, embracing a flexible strategy that results in a more innovative organization.

Leadership Education

The two most puzzling results in the empirical study are related to the educational level and educational diversity of the senior team. As noted previously, several empirical studies (Bantel and Jackson 1989; Wiersma and Bantel 1992) have found that leaders with higher levels of education are more open to different points of view and cognitive diversity can help offset the negative tendencies resulting from leaders existing for long periods in a single profession. In the innovation study, neither educational level nor educational diversity of the library leadership team had a significant impact on innovation performance (appendix C).

In this study, we also examined educational diversity as it relates to science degrees held by the senior team. Library leaders with diverse academic backgrounds and with degrees in science, engineering, and computer science are likely to be more supportive of technology-based innovations originating in these disciplines. The correlation of education diversity (science)[24] was small but positive, suggesting that senior teams with science degrees might have more of an impact on innovation performance.

---

[24] Educational diversity (science) was constructed by examining the number of science-related degrees that were held by the leadership team.

Reassessing Upper Echelons Theory

There is a continuing debate and dialog about the effectiveness of the upper echelons theory (Hambrick 2007). Organizational theorists have demonstrated early and persistent support for the upper echelons perspective in studies regarding the positive effect of elites' attitude toward change and innovation (Daft 1978; Damanpour and Aravind 2012; Hage and Dewar 1973). However, Edmondson, Roberto, and Watkins (2003) argue that the Top Management Team (TMT) demographic composition is relatively stable and does not account for specific situations. This lack of refinement or precision has led to conflicting empirical results due, in part, to the imperfect proxies inherent in the theoretical approach. Situational leadership research suggests that leaders will adjust their styles based on specific circumstances (Hersey, Blanchard, and Natemeyer 1979). In a specific situation, a leader may choose either a highly directive or a highly participative management style.

Finkelstein and Hambrick (1990) have examined managerial discretion as a possible bridge between these disparate theoretical approaches. Managerial discretion refers to the latitude of action available to top executives. From a methodological perspective, Hambrick (2007) has noted that upper echelons theory will have more explanatory power in organizations where managerial discretion is high. Finkelstein and Hambrick (1990) studied some 100 for-profit firms and found that executive team tenure had a stronger impact on firm performance when these executives had more managerial discretion. Finkelstein and Hambrick hypothesize that where discretion is high, upper echelons theory is likely to have stronger explanatory power.

This effect is quite intuitive. Given the oversight from the university and the librarian allegiance to the traditions and norms of the profession, leaders might have less autonomy to make independent decisions regarding major change. In fact, the parent institution—administrators, faculty advisory groups, and budget constraints—can restrict the autonomy of library leaders. Thus, the methodological perspective explains, in part, the low correlations of innovation performance with age and tenure in ARL libraries.

Conclusion

The lack of correlation between library leadership age and education, specifically science education, and innovation performance deserves more discussion. From the innovation study, it was apparent that the demographics of the library leadership team did not affect innovation performance. In an extensive meta-analysis of empirical research in the period from 1990 to 2009, Damanpour and Aravind (2012, 509) report that the impact of managers' age on innovation was nonsignificant and "the negative effect of tenure on innovation has been overstated in the literature." This in-depth analysis supports what we found in the ARL study as depicted in table 9.2, where both mature and young teams were shown to be innovative. Given that the library age profile will not change quickly, this observation suggests that research libraries can continue to innovate and benefit from the experience and professionalism of the more mature library leader.

However, leadership educational diversity remains a concern. In the coming years, the research library will be overwhelmed with advanced technologies that can be applied to create totally new services. Open-source software provides a rich source of new knowledge and high-quality software for library applications. Robotics and intelligent systems are advancing rapidly into virtually every aspect of society, and a library robot could probably handle many routine reference questions. Deep learning and the application of neural networks are resulting in major advances in acoustic modeling and image recognition, offering the potential to significantly benefit the use of library multimedia resources (Hinton et al. 2012). Online tutorials for bibliographic instruction hold promise for extending this valuable instruction to all those students who need it (Tancheva 2003). Although many of these technological breakthroughs will occur in the world's research labs, the library will need leaders and members who understand the technology, can transfer it into the library, and can apply it to new and existing services.

References

Bantel, Karen A., and Susan E. Jackson. 1989. "Top Management and Innovations in Banking: Does the Composition of the Top Team Make a Difference?" *Strategic Management Journal* 10 (May): 107–24.

Carmelo-Ordaz, Carmen, Ana Beatriz Hernández-Lara, and Ramón Valle-Cabrera. 2005. "The Relationship between Top Management Teams and Innovative Capacity in Companies." *Journal of Management Development* 24, no. 8: 683–705.

Daellenbach, Urs S., Anne M. McCarthy, and Timothy S. Schoenecker. 1999. "Commitment to Innovation: The Impact of Top Management Team Characteristics." *R&D Management* 29, no. 3 (July): 199–208.

Daft, Richard L. 1978. "A Dual-Core Model of Organizational Innovation." *Academy of Management Journal* 21, no. 2 (June): 193–210.

Daft, Richard L., and Selwyn W. Becker. 1978. *Innovation in Organizations: Innovation Adoption in School Organizations.* New York: Elsevier.

Damanpour, Fariborz, and Deepa Aravind. 2011. "Managerial Innovation: Conceptions, Processes, and Antecedents." *Management and Organization Review* 8, no. 2 (July): 423–54.

———. 2012. "Organizational Structure and Innovation Revisited: From Organic to Ambidextrous Structure." In *Handbook of Organizational Creativity,* edited by Michael D. Mumford, 483–513. Waltham, MA: Academic Press.

Damanpour, Fariborz, and Marguerite Schneider. 2009. "Characteristics of Innovation and Innovation Adoption in Public Organizations: Assessing the Role of Managers." *Journal of Public Administration Research and Theory* 19, no. 3: 495–522.

Davis, Carolyn D. 2003. "Organizational Innovation: The Role of Top Management in Different Stages of Innovation Implementation." PhD dissertation, Georgia Institute of Technology. ProQuest Dissertations & Theses: A&I (AAT 3110401).

Edmondson, Amy C., Michael A. Roberto, and Michael D. Watkins. 2003. "A Dynamic Model of Top Management Team Effectiveness: Managing Unstructured Task Streams." *Leadership Quarterly* 14, no. 3 (June): 297–325.

Fernández-Mesa, Anabel, María Iborra, and Vicente Safón. 2013. "CEO-TMT Interaction: Do Tenure and Age Affect Ambidexterity Dynamism?" *European Journal of International Management* 7, no. 1: 31–55.

Finkelstein, Sydney, and Donald C. Hambrick. 1990. "Top-Management-Team Tenure and Organizational Outcomes: The Moderating Role of Managerial Discretion." *Administrative Science Quarterly* 35, no. 3 (September): 484–503.

Hage, Jerald, and Robert Dewar. 1973. "Elite Values versus Organizational Structure in Predicting Innovation." *Administrative Science Quarterly* 18, no. 3 (September): 279–90.

Hambrick, Donald C. 1994. "Top Management Groups: A Conceptual Integration and Reconsideration of the 'Team' Label." In *Research in Organizational Behavior,* vol. 16, edited by Barry M. Staw and Larry L. Cummings, 171–213. Greenwich, CT: JAI Press.

———. 2007. "Upper Echelons Theory: An Update." *Academy of Management Review* 32, no. 2 (April): 334–43.

Hambrick, Donald C., and P. A. Manson. 1984. "Upper Echelons: The Organization as a Reflection of Its Top Managers." *Academy of Management Review* 9, no. 2 (April): 193–206.

Hersey, Paul, Kenneth H. Blanchard, and Walter E. Natemeyer. 1979. "Situational Leadership, Perception, and the Impact of Power." *Group and Organization Management* 4, no. 4 (December): 418–28.

Hinton, Geoffrey, Li Deng, Dong Yu, George Dahl, Abdel-rahman Mohamed, Navdeep Jaitly, Andrew Senior, Vincent Vanhoucke, Patrick Nguyen, Tara Sainath, and Brian Kingsbury. 2012. "Deep Neural Networks for Acoustic Modeling in Speech Recognition: The Shared Views of Four Research Groups." *IEEE Signal Processing Magazine* 29, no. 6: 82–97.

Koberg, Christine S., Dawn R. Detienne, and Kurt A. Heppard. 2003. "An Empirical Test of Environmental, Organizational, and Process Factors Affecting Incremental and Radical Innovation." *Journal of High Technology Management Research* 14, no. 1 (Spring): 21–45.

Tancheva, Kornelia. 2003. "Online Tutorials for Library Instruction: An Ongoing Project under Constant Revision." Presentation, ACRL 11th National Conference, Charlotte, NC, April 10–13. http://www.ala.org/acrl/sites/ala.org.acrl/files/content/conferences/pdf/tancheva.PDF.

Wiersema, Margarethe F., and Karen A. Bantel. 1992. "Top Management Team Demography and Corporate Strategic Change." *Academy of Management Journal* 35, no. 1 (March): 91–121.

Wilder, Stanley J. 1999. *The Age Demographics of Academic Librarians: A Profession Apart.* Binghamton, NY: Haworth Information Press.

Part Three
AN INNOVATIVE
CULTURE

Chapter 10

Management Innovations:
Creating the Innovative Culture

CULTURE CAN BE DEFINED as the deeply seated and often unconscious values and beliefs shared by the personnel in an organization (Martins and Terblanche 2003). In a historic and well-established institution, the culture acts in a way to preserve the status quo, making it very difficult to implement a major new innovation. The "iron cage" metaphor (DiMaggio and Powell 1983) accurately portrays this situation and suggests that the library institutional culture perpetuates some of the more restrictive aspects embedded in the norms and traditions of the profession. In these more bureaucratic organizations, "There's little room for passion, ingenuity, and self-direction" (Hamel 2006, 8), resulting in an inability to respond to a rapidly changing external environment that requires flexibility and creativity. In addition to Hamel's view of the corporate world, similar insights are emerging from academia. Much of what James Duderstadt writes about the university is relevant for research libraries. In what some would call a significant departure from conventional academic wisdom, he notes that "the forces of change upon the contemporary university, driven by social change, economic imperatives and technology, may be far beyond the capacity of our current educational paradigms" (Duderstadt 2000, 261).

The study of how future library leaders view their culture is revealing. Using the Competing Values Framework, Maloney and colleagues (2010) found that future library leaders viewed the library culture as primarily hierarchical with a focus on stability and the associated rules and procedures. These future leaders preferred a more innovative culture that could respond to both the disruptions and the opportunities emerging in the university and the external environment. To transform the library culture to one that is more open to change, leaders will need to expend considerable effort in an intense, iterative activity—communicating, sharing ideas, and articulating goals (Jelinek and Schoonhoven 1991, 84), ultimately taking the institution to a place that most of today's professional librarians have not experienced.

From the previous chapters, we have seen that an integrated leadership team, effective decision making, and a strategy that embraces flexibility are factors that can stimulate and sustain a more innovative culture in the library. The significant factors in the research model accounted for almost 50 percent of the variation in innovation performance of research libraries. Obviously, other factors in the complex social environment of the library can affect the ability to innovate. This chapter builds on the earlier empirical results to suggest that a new model for innovation is needed in the research library. This new model stresses the importance of management and administrative innovations in contrast to the technical innovation that is delivered to the end user.

Recent innovation research (Birkinshaw, Hamel, and Mol 2008) has begun to focus on management innovation, a promising new area that relates to the work of the organization—administrative practices, efficiency, organizational structure, and strategy. Hamel (2006, 4) defines management innovation as "a marked departure from traditional management principles, processes, and practices or a departure from customary organizational forms that significantly alter the way the work of management is performed." In his review of innovative business enterprises, Hamel highlights the need to challenge conventional management practices and to search for radical management principles. Wong's (2013) study demonstrated that management innovations affect critical dimensions of the work environment including human resources, process, and marketing. In a study of public libraries in six Northeast states, Damanpour and Evan (1984) found that the relationship between administrative and technical innovations is even more impacting in high-performance organizations. The premise in this text is that management innovations become the primary enablers of major change in the research library. This chapter reviews the theoretical underpinnings for these management and administrative innovations and discusses specific examples for library practitioners to consider.

Management Innovation

Major sources of management innovation are the managers themselves. However, these innovations do not result in new products or services for the end user. Rather, the innovation relates to how the organization does its work. In a recent study, Damanpour and Aravind (2011, 429) reviewed the changing vocabulary related to management and innovation and proposed an encompassing definition for managerial innovation that includes *"new approaches in knowledge for performing the work of management and new processes that produce changes in the organization's strategy, structure, administrative procedures, and systems"* (italics in original). Within these broad categories, one can imagine variants or subdivisions including innovations for marketing new products and services and approaches for collaborating across institutional boundaries, what Walker (2008) has called ancillary innovations. All of these innovations are important, not only for the efficient operation of the organization, but also for driving organizational change and renewal.

Birkinshaw, Hamel, and Mol (2008) discuss the various perspectives that have emerged in the research literature regarding management innovation. The perspectives and core questions are instructive for how management innovations might emerge in a research library. The *institutional perspective* addresses the various socioeconomic conditions that can give rise to or restrict management innovation. For the research library, the norms of the profession and the bureaucratic traditions of the university are part of the social environment that limits the organization's ability to innovate. As one example, the continuing decline of the library budget is part of the institutional and economic climate in which the library resides. The *cultural perspective* acknowledges that established organizations do not change easily, and there is considerable emphasis on preserving the status quo and avoiding the risks that might lead to radical innovations. The library focus on service quality and adherence to rules and processes is part of the culture that can resist major change. In a case study, Mc-Cabe (2002) examines how managers' subjectivity becomes embedded in the culture of an organization, resulting in resistance to a new way of doing things and perpetuating established practices. This cultural inertia typically results in incremental innovations and minor improvements to existing services (Jantz 2012). Conner's (2014, 147) recent case study of four academic libraries supports this view in reporting that most innovations are a repurposing of what is already there. The *rational perspective* is based on the notion that managers and leaders will recognize performance gaps and opportunities and will act to put in place more effective ways of working to address these issues.

The three perspectives provide clues as to how innovations might emerge in the library. Jolts from the external environment can cause a leader to take action, but the embedded culture can act against any change in order to preserve the status quo. Managers, however, do initiate innovations and they are not merely passive agents of the environment or subject to the restrictions of the established culture. Management innovations are frequently tacit and difficult to define and can take a long time to thoroughly diffuse throughout the organization (Birkinshaw, Hamel, and Mol 2008). Few professional librarians have formal training that prepares them to create these truly innovative management approaches. The focus on management innovation will require a reorientation in order to innovate in the critical dimensions of management practice including developing strategy, implementing R&D initiatives, managing human resources, building teams, making decisions, and tracking performance.

Stimulating Creativity and Ideas

The innovation process begins with creativity and how ideas are generated and preserved in the organization. Questions for library leadership relate to whether new ideas are being generated in sufficient numbers and how ideas are acted upon. These questions can be framed within the context of what Hansen and Birkinshaw (2007) have called the "innovation value chain"—idea generation, conversion, and diffusion. In a sense, it is a way of looking at the innovation diffusion process in figure 3.1 through the lens of idea generation (figure 10.1). Figure 10.1 is an oversimplification of a complex process in which an idea must gain currency and pass through increasingly resistant hurdles in order to become a successful innovation.

FIGURE 10.1
The Innovation Value Chain (adapted from Hansen and Birkinshaw 2007)

There is a key question for leaders and managers in each phase of the value chain. Are members of the library creating good ideas or bringing in good ideas from other organizations? Are the best of these ideas selected and acted upon in a timely fashion? Are the resulting innovations properly marketed and diffused throughout the targeted client base? Answers to these questions can provide possibilities for management innovations that will support the innate, creative talents of each member of the library.

Creativity is the "production of novel and useful ideas in any domain" (Amabile 1996, 1). Amabile's research highlights two major aspects of creativity in organizations. First, all humans with normal capacities can be creative and, secondly, the social environment can influence both the level and frequency of creative behavior. Ideas must surface within the organization and survive long enough to get the attention of library leadership. As Ekvall (1991, 73) points out, "idea management is about finding and taking care of ideas for change in the organization's operations, concerning both products and processes." Intuition, insights—what Johnson (2010, 77–78) calls hunches and describes as "fragile creatures" — take time to develop into ideas worthy of consideration.

At this early stage of idea generation and management, there must be people in the organization who can supply the energy necessary to raise the ideas to a threshold of organizational consciousness where discussion can begin (Van de Ven 1986, 592). The debate within the leadership team will be based not only on the merits of the idea but also on the compatibility of the potential innovation with the library mission and the difficulty of implementation. A primary role of leaders and managers is to provide the environment for stimulating new ideas, to champion the best ideas, and to provide the resources for implementation (Amabile 1998; Hansen and Birkinshaw 2007). This more creative library environment can be brought about by managers innovating, not in the realm of new product or service innovations, but rather in how the organization carries out its work. Process, structural, and strategic innovations can all move the organization towards a more creative culture. Specific examples of management innovations are highlighted here, each representing significant change in how the library does its work. For each, the management innovator will need to build legitimacy so that the innovation becomes acceptable to those constituencies that are impacted (Birkinshaw, Hamel, and Mol 2008).

Process Innovations

Process innovations can improve the efficiency of the organization, but these innovations can also stimulate new ideas through incentive systems or by putting in place approaches to generate and manage ideas.

An Idea Database

Do members of the research library generate ideas in sufficient quantities to support a more innovative culture? Alternatively, are library members bringing in new ideas from other organizations and from firms in the for-profit sector? In all likelihood, library leaders have only anecdotal evidence to answer this question. Variants of the idea database have been used by many of our most creative scientists. Joseph Priestly and Charles Darwin used their commonplace books "as a repository for a vast miscellany of hunches" (Johnson 2010, 86). An idea database can preserve hunches and ill-formed intuitions in order to provide the time for maturation into a well-formed idea. Although standard database tools can be used to collect and manage ideas, this more technological approach does not typically take into account the unique needs of library innovation.

Litchfield and Gilson (2013) have proposed an approach for the management of creativity that uses a museum metaphor for curating idea collections. The idea curators do not take responsibility for the ideas nor would they necessarily generate or develop work plans to support a particular idea. Relative to the earlier discussion on organizational ambidexterity, curators typically are seeking a strategic balance in their collections and will organize idea collections to support both exploitative and exploratory strategies. The activities of idea curators can be organized into three domains: shaping idea collections, maintaining idea collections, and getting the idea used and converted into viable new services. Shaping involves creating a balance with an appropriate mix of ideas that support the library's strategy. The maintaining function has the obvious roles of providing access to the collection but also deaccessing ideas that are no longer relevant. The activity of "using creative ideas" relates to the diffusion process by connecting an idea to a potentially innovative new service and moving it into the discussion, adoption, and implementation stages.

One of Litchfield and Gilson's most useful suggestions is for organizational members to study the idea collections to understand what ideas have worked, how various ideas can be integrated to form a totally new innovation and to insure that the idea database does not become some forgotten archive. These researchers have combined the curator function with idea management to create a unique new role for research libraries and one that fits nicely with the traditions and culture of the library. This role can easily be extended by transforming the idea database into a learning forum in which ideas are discussed with members of the organization to enhance learning and the growth of knowledge. As Fowler (1998) reports, there is evidence in academic libraries that this continuous learning is a critical foundation for innovation.

In the corporate world, the best innovators have systematized the generation and testing of new ideas. Hargadon and Sutton (2000) report that two major techniques have been successful in the commercial sector. First, there is the concept of knowledge brokering, in which organization members serve as intermediaries between disconnected pools of ideas. These people are constantly scavenging for old ideas within the organization that can be reapplied in new contexts. Secondly, these brokers keep old ideas alive by communicating across the organization and talking about how these ideas might be applied in different areas. Johnson (2010, 61) notes that the most productive tool for generating good ideas is the "circle of humans, at a table, talking shop." Klein and Convertino (2014, 40) report a variant on this approach that can augment the generation of new ideas. Major corporations such as IBM and Starbucks have used crowdsourcing to solve a particular problem. "Crowds can rapidly develop huge volumes of novel ideas by recombining and refining the ideas proposed by other participants."

In effect, the idea database becomes an information exchange and knowledge management tool, facilitating the growth of individual and organizational intelligence. The idea database helps answer the question in the first stage of the value chain about whether sufficient new ideas are forthcoming from within the organization. Assuming there is consensus about proceeding to the next stage in the value chain, a leader or leaders must step forward to support the idea and guide it through an organizational maze—some would call this a "gauntlet"—in order for the idea to move through the idea conversion and diffusion stages of the value chain.

Human Resources

Human resource (HR) practices are critical in order to provide an organizational climate that fosters creativity and critical thinking. These practices, such as employee training, performance appraisal, and reward systems, do not directly affect organizational performance but rather work through other processes, including administrative practices and technical innovation, to enhance the performance of the organization (Ceylan 2013; Chen and Huang 2009).

Scarbrough (2003) characterizes HR management as the intersection of two flows: people flow and knowledge flow. Careful selection of people for a project, establishing innovative compensation strategies, and revising career and performance appraisal systems can all improve the flow of knowledge throughout the organization—how this knowledge is acquired, how it is shared, and how it is applied to solve problems.

Employees should have an understanding that expressing their thoughts and ideas will not jeopardize their career or status in the organization. For radical innovation to occur and flourish, the organization and HR practices must provide psychological safety. By defining predictors of organization-level practices and team-based practices, Un (2010) found that the organizational-based approach offers more psychological safety and therefore supports radical innovations more effectively while the focus on team practices is better for achieving incremental innovations.

Performance appraisal is probably one of the most challenging HR tasks for managers, the least effective for improving individual performance, and one that creates more dissatisfaction among organizational members than any other management process. The research library generally follows the procedures established by the university HR organization in terms of how to do performance review. However, there are complementary procedures that can be put in place to improve the process.

For example, to emphasize the customer-supplier relationship, each organizational member can identify customers who are recipients of his or her work during the performance year. These "customers" can be peers, subordinates, or managers within the organization or others within or external to the university. The customer uses a form to address the quality, reliability, and timeliness of the service and also provides a free-text assessment of the individual's performance. These forms are anonymous and are provided to the employee's administrative manager for review.[25] In a subsequent meeting with the employee, the manager reviews the forms with the employee and discusses possibilities for improvement. In the end, the employee receives more direct and credible feedback from those who are intimately familiar with the quality of their work. As Ceylan (2013) points out, HR practices can enhance human capital creativity by improving morale and providing more constructive feedback to the employee.

Obviously, the HR strategy is closely connected to and dependent on the senior leadership team. Collins and Clark (2003) have found that the social network of the senior team can mediate the relationship between HR practices and the performance of technology-based firms. In effect, integration of the team at the top of the organization strengthens the impact of HR practices, resulting in better organizational performance.

New Roles

The HR function is closely associated with the creation of new roles in the library. As libraries innovate and introduce new services, marketing of these services becomes even more important (Spalding and Wang 2006). In discussing the opportunities for libraries in educational technology, Wolpert (1998, 33) emphasized the role of marketing: "Libraries must become substantially more sophisticated about packaging, advertising, and promoting their valuable resources." In a study of organizations in a US government agency, Hurley and Hult (1998) report that a market orientation can enhance performance when it is combined with organizational learning—the development of new knowledge. Marketing can help the organization anticipate user needs whereas organizational learn-

---

[25] The author has been involved with a similar process in his earlier work at Bell Laboratories and found that the approach provided a significant improvement over more traditional performance appraisal processes.

ing helps the organization translate these needs into innovative services. Closely related to marketing is the role of looking outward and boundary spanning. Most of the technology for innovations will originate in the for-profit sector. Librarians can actively seek out and transfer this technology into the library where it can be modified and adapted by those involved with library R&D.

Managing Library R&D

Organizational structure and the creation of a separate R&D unit continue to be debated within the research library community. However, the benefits of exploration—the generation and use of new knowledge—cannot be overstated. Although the librarian profession can be considered "information intensive," as Neal (2006, 1) points out, it is an information-poor profession where "decisions are not supported by evidence" and "research in the field is poorly understood, communicated, and applied." In a classic paper, Cohen and Levinthal (1990) observe that an increased R&D investment creates a capacity to assimilate and exploit new knowledge that, in turn, enhances the innovativeness of the organization. Damanpour and Aravind (2012, 508) report that separating the allocation of resources for knowledge acquisition from those for operational activities can best support the R&D activity.

Many ideas result from exploratory work, and research libraries undertake R&D work in a variety of ways. However, relatively few research libraries have created separate R&D units. In the recent ARL Innovation SPEC Kit, the authors (German and Namachchivaya 2013, 16) report that 31 libraries have invested in R&D. However, only nine of these libraries have separate R&D units. The following quote characterizes how the other 22 libraries conduct R&D: "There is no formal staff or structure" and leaders "want the organization to be flexible enough to allow for different units to engage in R&D activities as necessary" (16). This more traditional approach to R&D significantly reduces the benefits that can accrue from exploratory work. First, embedding exploratory activities within a specific unit will likely produce incremental innovations that are specific to the functioning of that unit. Secondly, it is very difficult for an individual within one of these units to ascertain how much time he or she is allowed to spend on exploratory activities. Ultimately, whatever time has been approved yields to the priority and urgency to support existing services.[26] Finally, it is very difficult for library leaders to manage and assess the exploratory work that is distributed throughout the organization. These factors all speak to the advantages of creating a separate R&D unit or work group with considerable autonomy and ample financial resources.

In the ARL study, 15 libraries in the sample of 50 indicated that they had separate units for R&D work.[27] Yet, only eight of these libraries scored above the mean for innovative performance. Although it is difficult to draw any conclusions from this observation, it does suggest that research libraries are beginning to restructure in order to support more exploratory work, but are having difficulty integrating exploratory output into the services delivered to clients. Two important questions emerge for library leaders regarding exploratory work: (*a*) how do R&D activities become an integral part of the library culture and (*b*) what are the skills required to manage R&D activities?

Vision, Mission, and Strategy

An innovation strategy is one that will promote the development and implementation of new products and services. In her study of organizational effectiveness in colleges and universities, Cameron (1986) found that both management strategies and environmental dimensions were most important, highlighting proactive strategies with an external focus as being especially relevant. In a study of user-centered libraries, Deiss (2004) highlights the challenge to library leaders to utilize strategy to make decisions about innovations in order to create value-added services on a continuous basis. Conner (2014, 46) suggests that the way forward requires a redefinition of the library mission. The challenge to institutional leadership is to mobilize those strategic actions that will create the environment for more radical management innovation (Markides 1997).

---

[26] The author has extensive experience with this phenomenon in managing software development at Bell Laboratories. Members of technical staff were permitted to engage in R&D work for one day per week, but the press of development schedules rarely allowed them to take advantage of this time.

[27] This determination was made based on agreement from statement 10 on the survey: "In our library, exploratory and production activities are structurally separated" (Jantz 2013).

Support for Innovation

It has been shown in an extensive meta-analysis that a simple strategic statement supporting major change and innovation and communicated throughout the organization leads to a more innovative organization (Damanpour and Aravind 2012, 509). To further understand research library support of innovation, the strategic plans of all 50 ARL libraries in the study sample were examined to determine if innovation was a key element of library strategy. In the sample of 50 libraries, 17 had such a statement in their strategic plan. To qualify, the statement had to demonstrate an understanding of the difficulty of innovating and a commitment to making it happen. One of the best statements is as follows:

> In order to foster innovation in library service, (the library) must acknowledge the need for innovation, support the time required for it, and recognize that the time crunch can have a significant impact on the employee's ability to come up with creative solutions to problems in the library. (MSU Libraries 2008, 16)

For purposes of comparison, statements that did not qualify revealed an unconvincing commitment to innovation with little understanding of organizational complexity and the resulting conflicts. The following is an example of an unconvincing commitment to innovation from one ARL library: "Our mission is to inspire innovation and advance the ways knowledge is shared and preserved for posterity."

The Innovation Portfolio

Given the risk and uncertainty, the decision to adopt a major innovation and proceed with implementation cannot be taken lightly. Walker (2008) has identified a characteristic in nonprofits that seek legitimacy by claiming to have implemented an innovation. In the research library, a website might identify a new service that the library is offering. A specific librarian or workgroup might be charged with implementing this service while also coping with a diverse portfolio of other responsibilities. As a result, a potential new service can remain largely as a statement on the website or a prototype without sufficient resources to achieve full implementation. Unfinished prototypes, however, should not become a way of life. This risk can be mitigated and effectively managed through the use of an innovation portfolio. Library leaders can define and manage an innovation portfolio through the use of an innovation matrix that has two major benefits: (a) it gives managers a framework for reviewing all innovation initiatives that are underway and (b) the matrix also provides a mechanism to assess the mix of innovations that can be spread across core services, new services, and breakthroughs that are transformational for the library (Nagji and Tuff 2012). The balance across these three areas can be aligned with the library strategy in order to meet demands of clients while also incurring an acceptable amount of risk. The R&D Project Portfolio Matrix is one such specific tool for aligning with strategy and identifying gaps between possible long-term benefits and customer value (Mikkola 2001).

Conclusion

Mol and Birkinshaw (2006, 26) state that management innovation is "the missing piece of the innovation puzzle." The premise in this chapter is that management innovation is not only the primary driver of technical innovations but it is also needed to create a more innovative library culture—a key to thriving in the future. The discussion in this chapter has provided practical examples of innovation in several areas—process, organizational structure, and strategy. The innovation portfolio provides a mechanism for managers to understand the totality of their innovation program whereas the idea database and an R&D unit are process and structural approaches for generating and implementing new ideas. Finally, an innovation strategy—articulated and communicated—can create an atmosphere of freedom and empowerment for all organizational members to express and act on their ideas. Given the forces in the university that act to preserve the status quo, management innovations and management innovators become essential in order to effect major change in the research library.

References

Amabile, Teresa M. 1996. "Creativity and Innovation in Organizations." Harvard Business School Background Note, 396-239 (January).

———. 1998. "How to Kill Creativity." *Harvard Business Review* 76, no. 5 (September): 77–87.

Birkinshaw, Julian, Gary Hamel, and Michael J. Mol. 2008. "Management Innovation." *Academy of Management Review* 33, no. 4 (October): 825–45.

Cameron, K. 1986. "A Study of Organizational Effectiveness and Its Predictors." *Management Science* 32, no. 1 (January): 87–112.

Ceylan, Canan. 2013. "Commitment-Based HR Practices, Different Types of Innovation Activities and Firm Innovation Performance." *International Journal of Human Resource Management* 24, no. 1: 208–26.

Chen, Chung-Jen, and Jing-Wen Huang. 2009. "Strategic Human Resource Practices and Innovation Performance: The Mediating Role of Knowledge Management Capacity." *Journal of Business Research* 62, no. 1 (January): 104–14.

Cohen, Wesley M., and Daniel A. Levinthal. 1990. "Absorptive Capacity: A New Perspective on Learning and Innovation." *Administrative Science Quarterly* 35, no. 1 (March): 128–52.

Collins, Christopher J., and Kevin D. Clark. 2003. "Strategic Human Resource Practices, Top Management Team Social Networks, and Firm Performance: The Role of Human Resource Practices in Creating Organizational Competitive Advantage." *Academy of Management Journal* 48, no. 6 (December): 740–51.

Conner, Matthew. 2014. *The New University Library: Four Case Studies.* Chicago: American Library Association.

Damanpour, Fariborz, and Deepa Aravind. 2011. "Managerial Innovation: Conceptions, Processes, and Antecedents." *Management and Organization Review* 8, no. 2 (July): 423–54.

———. 2012. "Organizational Structure and Innovation Revisited: From Organic to Ambidextrous Structure." In *Handbook of Organizational Creativity*, edited by Michael D. Mumford, 483–513. Waltham, MA: Academic Press.

Damanpour, Fariborz, and William M. Evan. 1984. "Organizational Innovation and Performance: The Problem of 'Organizational Lag.'" *Administrative Science Quarterly* 29, no. 3 (September): 392–409.

Deiss, Kathryn. 2004. "Innovation and Strategy: Risk and Choice in Shaping User-Centered Libraries." *Library Trends* 53, no. 1: 17–32. http://hdl.handle.net/2142/1717.

DiMaggio, Paul J., and Walter W. Powell. 1983. "The Iron Cage Revisited: Institutional Isomorphism and Collective Rationality in Organizational Fields." *American Sociological Review* 48, no. 2: 147–160.

Duderstadt, James J. 2000. *A University for the 21st Century.* Ann Arbor: University of Michigan Press.

Ekvall, G. 1991. "The Organizational Culture of Idea-Management: A Creative Climate for the Management of Ideas." In *Managing Innovation*, edited by Jane Henry and David Walker, 73–79. London: Sage Publications.

Fowler, Rena K. 1998. "The University Library as Learning Organization for Innovation: An Exploratory Study." *College and Research Libraries* 59, no. 3 (May): 220–31.

German, Lisa, and Beth Sandore Namachchivaya. 2013. *Innovation and R&D: SPEC Kit 339.* Washington, DC: Association of Research Libraries.

Hamel, Gary. 2006. "The Why, What and How of Management Innovation." *Harvard Business Review* 84, no. 2 (February): 72–84.

Hansen, Morten T., and Julian Birkinshaw. 2007. "The Innovation Value Chain." *Harvard Business Review* 85, no. 6 (June): 121–30.

Hargadon, Andrew, and Robert I. Sutton. 2000. "Building an Innovation Factory." *Harvard Business Review* 78, no. 3 (May–June): 157–66.

Hurley, Robert F., and Tomas M. Hult. 1998. "Innovation, Market Orientation, and Organizational Learning: An Integration and Empirical Examination." *Journal of Marketing* 62, no. 3 (July): 42–54.

Jantz, Ronald C. 2012. "Innovation in Academic Libraries: An Analysis of University Librarians' Perspectives." *Library and Information Science Research* 34, no. 1 (January): 3–12. doi:10.1016/j.lisr.2011.07.008.

———. 2013. "Incremental and Radical Innovations—Survey," May 20, doi:10.7282/T37D2S88.

Jelinek, Mariann, and Claudia Bird Schoonhoven. 1991. "Strong Culture and its Consequences." In *Managing Innovation,* edited by Jane Henry and David Walker, 80–88. London: Sage Publications.

Johnson, Steven. 2010. *Where Good Ideas Come From.* New York: Riverside Books.

Klein, Mark, and Gregorio Convertino. 2014. "An Embarrassment of Riches: A Critical Review of Open Innovation Systems." *Communications of the ACM* 57, no. 11: 40–42.

Litchfield, Robert C., and Lucy L. Gilson. 2013. "Curating Collections of Ideas: Museum as Metaphor in the Management of Creativity." *Industrial Marketing Management* 42, no. 1 (January): 106–12.

Maloney, Krisellen, Kristin Antelman, Kenning Arlitsch, and John Butler. 2010. "Future Leaders' Views on Organizational Culture." *College and Research Libraries* 71, no. 4 (July): 322–47. doi:10.5860/crl-47.

Markides, Constantinos. 1997. "Strategic Innovation," *Sloan Management Review* 38, no. 3 (Spring): 9–23.

Martins, E. C., and F. Terblanche. 2003. "Building Organisational Culture That Stimulates Creativity and Innovation." *European Journal of Innovation Management* 6, no. 1: 64–74.

McCabe, Darren. 2002. "'Waiting for Dead Men's Shoes': Towards a Cultural Understanding of Management Innovation." *Human Relations* 55, no. 5 (May): 505–36.

Mikkola, Juliana Hsuan. 2001. "Portfolio Management of R&D Projects: Implications for Innovation Management." *Technovation* 21, no. 7 (July): 423–35.

Mol, Michael J., and Julian M. Birkinshaw. (2006). "Against the Flow: Reaping the Rewards of Management Innovation." *European Business Forum* 27 (Winter): 25–29.

MSU Libraries. 2008. *Vision Task Force Report.* East Lansing: Michigan State University Libraries. http://img.lib.msu.edu/about/VisionTaskForceReport.pdf.

Nagji, Bansi, and Geoff Tuff. 2012. "Managing Your Innovation Portfolio." *Harvard Business Review,* May: 67–74.

Neal, James G. 2006. "The Research and Development Imperative in the Academic Library: Path to the Future." *portal: Libraries and the Academy* 6, no. 1 (January): 1–3. doi: 10.7916/D8S75DF8.

Scarbrough, Harry. 2003. "Knowledge Management, HRM and Innovation Process." *International Journal of Manpower* 24, no. 5: 501–16.

Spalding, Helen H., and Jian Wang. 2006. "The Challenges and Opportunities of Marketing Academic Libraries in the USA." *Library Management* 27, no. 6/7 (June): 494–504.

Un, C. Annique. 2010. "An Empirical Multi-level Analysis for Achieving Balance between Incremental and Radical Innovations." *Journal of Engineering and Technology Management* 27, no. 1–2 (March–June): 1–19.

Van de Ven, Andrew H. 1986. "Central Problems in the Management of Innovation." *Management Science* 32, no. 5 (May): 590–607.

Walker, Richard M. 2008. "An Empirical Evaluation of Innovation Types and Organizational and Environmental Characteristics: Towards a Configuration Framework." *Journal of Public Administration Research and Theory* 18, no. 4: 591–615.

Wolpert, Ann. 1998. "Services to Remote Users: Marketing the Library's Role." *Library Trends* 47, no. 1 (Summer): 21–41.

Wong, Stanley Kam Sing. 2013. "The Role of Management Involvement in Innovation." *Management Decision* 51, no. 4: 709–29.

Chapter 11

The Singular Leader, Radical Innovations, and For-Profit Firms

IN THE EARLIER CHAPTERS, we set out the innovation framework to be used in this study with a discussion of innovation types and the innovation diffusion process. Our study revealed the importance of senior team integration, an ambidextrous and flexible organization, and clarity of the decision process. At this juncture, we have some considerable insight based on empirical analysis that these factors can lead to a more innovative library. In chapter ten, we further examined the importance of management innovations as an essential prerequisite to insure the success of technical innovations, taking the opportunity to suggest possibilities for library leaders to consider.

In this chapter, we further exploit the underlying data from survey respondents to reveal other possible factors that might affect innovation in the research library. The research model enabled us to view the library as an organization through the eyes of the leadership team. The data from these respondents also offers the opportunity to further explore possibilities related to the singular leader and radical innovations.

The Singular Leader

The study of organizational leadership requires one to examine both the leadership team and the singular leader. Leaders can encourage innovative activities as a pathway to an effective organization. Although the singular

145

leader is a member of the integrated management team, she is also likely to have a strategic vision and unique skills that are essential for managing in a more turbulent environment.

Hambrick and Manson (1984) suggested that organizations reflect the values of their leaders. The singular leader can reorient the organization to one that can adapt to a dynamic and rapidly changing environment, championing and actively supporting an innovation through the various diffusion stages of the innovation process. The singular leader may be the one who advocates for taking on more risk and who has the authority and credibility to overcome organizational resistance to undertake the implementation of major innovations.

Past research has demonstrated that innovation adoption is affected by the individual leader's values and attitudes (Moon and deLeon 2001; Rivera, Streib, and Willoughby 2000). Moon and deLeon's research investigated US municipal governments with a focus on "reinventing government," a process that has challenges similar to transforming the research library. Findings from this research indicated that the chief administrator's reinvention values were positively associated with the adoption of reinvention programs. Researchers have examined the pro-innovation attitude of leaders in nonprofit organizations and found that this attitude in the singular leader is positively associated with innovation adoption (Daft and Becker 1978; Damanpour and Schneider 2009).

The leader's opinions about which innovations to pursue will have more weight in the decision process while the singular leader's social skills will be important to promote innovative ideas throughout the organization and to provide a supportive environment (Axtell et al. 2000). The leader's positive view of the institution's ability to create innovative products will be expected to permeate throughout the organization, empowering members to be more innovative and stimulating related practices such as brainstorming sessions, informal discussions, and increased conference attendance.

The Library Director's Attitude toward Major Change

Given these findings, it was expected that the library director's attitude with respect to major change and innovation would impact innovation performance in the research library. The centralized structure of the research library and the traditions of the institutional nonprofit give considerable power and authority to the singular leader. Thus, it is reasonable to expect that the university librarian[28] as an individual will have a significant impact on the innovation performance of the library.

The questions in the ARL survey regarding the exploratory and exploitative activities of the library provide an opportunity to examine the singular leader's attitude toward innovation. The view of the singular leader was constructed from the university librarian's responses to the six statements concerning exploratory work in the library.[29] A sample statement requiring agreement on a nine-point Likert scale was as follows: "Your library looks for novel product and service ideas by thinking outside the box." The responses from the six statements were averaged to form a single indicator—*singular leader attitude*. The resulting perspectives from library leaders were positively correlated with innovation performance ($r = 0.24$, $p < .05$, $n = 50$; see the *singular leader attitude*—LDR variable, appendix C). By dichotomizing the director's response for exploratory support and innovation performance, the impact of the leader's support for exploratory activities on innovation is dramatically illustrated in table 11.1.

TABLE 11.1
The Singular Leader Attitude toward Exploratory Work (*N* = 50)

	Innovative Libraries	Non-innovative Libraries	Total
More Supportive of Exploratory Work	19	8	27
Less Supportive of Exploratory Work	8	15	23
Total	27	23	50

Although we can't claim a causal relationship between the singular leader attitude and innovation performance, table 11.1 and the correlation suggest that there is 95 percent probability of a real relationship between these two variables. As the shaded cells indicate, 19 of the ARL libraries with leaders who support exploratory work were also innovative,

---

[28] The phrases *university librarian* and *director* will be used interchangeably as the designation for the singular leader in the research library.

[29] See questions 21–26 on the ARL survey (Jantz 2013).

whereas 15 ARL libraries whose leaders were not as supportive were not innovative. There is also a significant relationship between the singular leader attitude and the integration of the senior team ($r = 0.26, p < .05, n = 50$), suggesting that library directors with a pro-innovation perspective are also likely to lead more integrated teams.

Singular Leader Age

In a seminal paper on upper echelons theory, Hambrick and Manson (1984) put forth several reasons why the age of leaders will affect performance outcomes in an organization. Older executives have a greater commitment to the status quo and may be at a point in their lives in which financial and career security has become very important. Thus, incurring risk to embark on a major radical innovation becomes less likely. There are, however, countervailing views that suggest the older leader has a tendency to seek more information and to evaluate it more accurately.

The aging library profession provided the impetus in this study to examine the impact of the more mature library leader on the innovativeness of the library. However, we did not find a significant correlation between the director's age and innovation performance. Table 11.2 provides a view of how the more mature and younger ARL directors affected innovation performance in their libraries. Although mature directors are evident in equal numbers for innovative and non-innovative libraries, we do see a difference for young leaders. Twelve innovative libraries were led by young leaders, versus eight non-innovative libraries led by young directors.

TABLE 11.2 Singular Leader Age and Innovation (N = 48)			
	Innovative Libraries	Non-innovative Libraries	Total
Mature Leaders	14	14	28
Young Leaders	12	8	20
Total	26	22	48[*]
* Ages were available for only 48 of the 50 responding ARL directors.			

Clearly, the theory regarding age demographics is yielding mixed results, and more research is required before one can conclude that the aging profession is having a negative impact on innovation in research libraries.

Radical Innovations

Jim Neal (2001, 12) has advocated for a more entrepreneurial library organization, stating that "it will require a redefinition of the physical, expertise, and intellectual infrastructure, and a new understanding of the geography, psychology and economics of innovation.... *And it will mean advancing from incremental to radical change*" [author's italics].

In the ARL study, we constructed an innovation performance metric that included an assessment of the library's ability to implement both incremental and radical innovations. Libraries that were good innovators demonstrated a balance of both incremental and radical innovations. Major change in libraries, however, will require the initiation and implementation of the more radical innovation. These innovations will alter library organizational structures and impact the organization's skills profile, requiring librarians and staff who can readily apply technological advancements within the library. The opportunity is not only to provide valuable new services to users but also to partner with the parent institution, becoming more than an information service provider for the university. In table 11.3, we constructed a variable, *radical innovation performance,* that assessed library performance based only on the organization's ability to implement the radical innovations shown in appendix A.

TABLE 11.3
Significant Correlations with Radical Innovation (*N* = 50)

Independent Variable	Correlation with Radical Innovation Performance
Team Behavior and Leadership	
Behavioral integration	0.35[a]
Decision awareness	0.38[a]
Singular leader attitude	0.25[b]
Organizational Strategy	
Ambidextrous orientation	0.43[a]
Organization	
Library Size (FTE)	0.42[a]

[a] Significant (1-tailed) at .01 level, [b] Significant at .05 level

As most readers would expect, the size of the library was significantly related to the ability of the library to implement radical innovations. Typically, the larger libraries will have more slack funds and are therefore able to undertake more risky projects. The other four factors dealing with team behavior, leadership, and organizational strategy all have a significant correlation with radical innovation performance.

To enter this new world of radical innovations, leaders will need to think deeply about the fundamental changes in the university and research library world and look for opportunities to exploit the emerging discontinuities. For successful implementation, the radical innovation will require extensive communication and marketing and the resolution of contentious internal issues such as where a new service should be placed organizationally. Undertaking radical innovations will produce more failures than with the routine incremental innovations, and the results will be less predictable. Innovation is about change. It therefore becomes necessary to understand what is changing and what is changing rapidly in the university. To take advantage of this change, library dogmas and mental models will need to be challenged in order to embrace the more radical innovation.

Learning from the For-Profit Experience

Throughout the discussion on innovation in research libraries, we have used theory and empirical results from the for-profit sector that might be applicable to the library. Clearly, the nonprofit and the research library are quite different organizations from for-profit firms. Discerning library leaders, however, can benefit from the lessons in surviving and thriving in corporate America. The author's personal experience at AT&T provides insight into the challenge of cultural change that is facing the research library.

Cultural Change and the AT&T Experience

Prior to the divestiture in 1984, the regulated AT&T was in some respects similar to the environment surrounding the research library. In 1913, AT&T agreed to become a regulated monopoly. The federal government, the "parent" of the corporation, guaranteed AT&T a rate of return based on the value of plant and equipment in exchange for reasonable customer rates and a commitment to serving a very large customer base. After deregulation and a surge in competition, AT&T saw its share of the long distance market drop below 60 percent and continue in a persistent decline. In 2005, Southwestern Bell Company purchased what remained of AT&T, including the name, and was able to forge a new direction that has proved successful. Underscoring the fragility of organizational life, O'Reilly, Harreld, and Tushman (2009) report that only 160 of 1,008 large, for-profit firms survived from 1962 to 1998.

The experiences and values of AT&T corporate leaders were formed in the traditional regulatory culture, leading to an inability to conceive of a quite different company. AT&T's greatest challenge was in changing the culture and psychology of its people, from "we have time to do things the way we think best" to "we have to compete in the market … and do so rapidly." Bringing about this transformation requires radical action through organizational structure, technology, and individual effort in order to render major change real and durable (Schneider, Brief, and Guzzo 1996).

Research library leaders are faced with an environment similar to that of the regulated AT&T in which annual funding is secure but also continues to decline. However, Schneider, Brief, and Guzzo (1996) suggest that a crisis may be needed in order to bring about radical change. With AT&T, the crisis was embodied in divestiture and significant loss of market share. For the library, the crisis is much more subtle and slow-moving, allowing more complacency and lack of action within the leadership team. Although mortality and bankruptcy are not in store for the library, similar forces can result in a decline to a much-reduced presence in the university. As in AT&T, it is likely that library leaders immersed in the profession and long in tenure will find it difficult to unlearn several decades of experience and imagine a quite different research library.

Traditional versus New Services

Similar to the for-profit sector, libraries have faced a quandary in how to support traditional services while also forging new directions. Marketing researchers have addressed the competitive issues of for-profit firms, examining factors that might lead to radical innovations. Chandy and Tellis (1998) studied firms that are willing to cannibalize existing products, suggesting that these actions are powerful drivers of radical innovations. The term *cannibalization* implies a marketing strategy in which a firm intentionally reduces the sales or market share of an existing product in order to introduce a new technology and a totally new product. Hermann, Tomczak, and Befurt (2006) found that the willingness to abandon current investments strongly determines radical product innovations. In a sense, various parts of the organization are competing against themselves. As noted earlier, Jesse Shera (1971, 64) has cited a similar library situation in which traditionalists and innovators are at odds with each other to the detriment of the library profession. While the traditionalists preserve and support existing services, the innovators may be willing to "cannibalize" or defund an existing service in order to provide resources to develop totally new capabilities.

Library Performance and Effectiveness

The nature of a nonprofit organization such as the research library is substantially different from that of the for-profit manufacturing or service firm. The goal of the nonprofit is to advance the public good and the ultimate product is "a changed human being" (Drucker 1990, xiv). Drucker (1990, 107) asks rhetorically, "What is the bottom line when there is no bottom line?" suggesting that nonprofit institutions do not have reliable methods to track performance.

How does innovation contribute to performance and is an innovative library also effective? If the mission and goals of the research library produce significant value and outcomes for the university, then tracking performance, reporting multi-year trends, and improving performance become important tasks for the library. While university provosts have agreed with the importance of collecting and reporting impact data, these senior administrators do not have specific ideas on how to obtain this data (Robertson 2015).

There is considerable evidence suggesting that an innovative organization will also perform well (Salge and Vera 2012). Researchers have proposed various models or frameworks for understanding effectiveness and performance in nonprofit organizations. Scholars have long debated how organizational effectiveness can be defined for a nonprofit (Forbes 1998; Kaplan 2001; Mitchell 2012). This earlier research suggests that organizational performance is best represented as a multidimensional construct consisting of both objective and subjective measures (Cameron 1981; Damanpour and Evan 1984; Herman and Renz 2008; Kaplan 2001; Matthews 2011). For many in the library and university community, clear and meaningful impact data are as yet an unattainable goal.

Achieving annual goals as one metric leaves open many questions regarding efficiency, financial management, and impact. In addition to goal attainment, performance categories include management effectiveness, input/output metrics, stakeholder perspectives, and strategic directions. Several questions are posed here that have been motivated by the political atmosphere in the university and issues related to tuition, student debt, and competition from for-profit universities. Are more quantitative performance indicators appropriate for a research library, and what might these indicators look like? Is it best for the research library to create and manage to performance indicators in order to avoid more onerous indicators that might be imposed from the external environment? How does the innovativeness of the library relate to overall organizational effectiveness? Will past performance drive future innovativeness, and will today's innovative organization result in future superior performance (Bowen, Rostami, and Steel 2010)?

Conclusion

We have hinted that libraries can learn from corporate America. Certain business practices such as defining effectiveness and tracking performance might serve the institution well in the transformational journey. The challenge will be to adopt useful corporate practices while also creating and communicating a hybrid model that preserves the mission and values of the research library. The transformation to a different organizational culture and climate will require a huge amount of time and energy, focusing on hierarchy, decision making, the nature of relationships, employee reward systems, and organizational structures.

The impact of the singular leader and the demonstrated benefits of the integrated senior team suggest that the library director's work might shift in focus. In the realm of the more innovative library, the singular leader can take advantage of the unique skills in the leadership team while also removing barriers to innovation. In a more contentious environment, debating the value of traditional services versus potential innovations, decisions and decision awareness become increasingly important as demonstrated in part by the positive effect of decision awareness (figure 5.2). Even in the more democratic environment of the library, many key decisions cannot be decided by voting. The library director, in the end, will need to avoid this decision paralysis. Finally, her actions in communicating, encouraging, and empowering can become transformative, capturing the energy, creativity, and commitment of all organizational members.

References

Axtell, C. M., D. J. Holman, K. L. Unsworth, T. D. Wall, P. E. Waterson, and E. Harrington. 2000. "Shopfloor Innovation: Facilitating the Suggestion and Implementation of Ideas." *Journal of Occupational and Organizational Psychology* 73, no. 3 (September): 265–85.

Bowen, Frances E., Mahdi Rostami, and Piers Steel. 2010. "Timing Is Everything: A Meta-analysis of the Relationships between Organizational Performance and Innovation." *Journal of Business Research* 63, no. 11 (November): 1179–85.

Cameron, Kim S. 1981. "Domains of Organizational Effectiveness in Colleges and Universities." *Academy of Management Journal* 24, no. 1 (March): 25–47.

Chandy, Rajesh K., and Gerard J. Tellis. 1998. "Organizing for Radical Product Innovation: The Overlooked Role of Willingness to Cannibalize." *Journal of Marketing Research* 35, no. 4 (November): 474–87.

Daft, Richard L., and Selwyn W. Becker. 1978. *Innovation in Organizations: Innovation Adoption in School Organizations.* New York: Elsevier.

Damanpour, Fariborz, and William M. Evan. 1984. "Organizational Innovation and Performance: The Problem of 'Organizational Lag.'" *Administrative Science Quarterly* 29, no. 3 (September): 392–409.

Damanpour, Fariborz, and Marguerite Schneider. 2009. "Characteristics of Innovation and Innovation Adoption in Public Organizations: Assessing the Role of Managers." *Journal of Public Administration Research and Theory* 19, no. 3: 495–522.

Drucker, Peter F. 1990. *Managing the Nonprofit Organization: Practices and Principles.* New York: HarperCollins.

Forbes, Daniel P. 1998. "Measuring the Unmeasurable: Empirical Studies of Nonprofit Organization Effectiveness from 1977 to 1997." *Nonprofit and Voluntary Sector Quarterly* 27, no. 2 (June): 183–202.

Hambrick, Donald C., and P. A. Manson. 1984. "Upper Echelons: The Organization as a Reflection of Its Top Managers." *Academy of Management Review* 9, no. 2 (April): 193–206.

Herman and Renz 2008. "Advancing Nonprofit Organizational Effectiveness Research and Theory." *Nonprofit Management and Leadership* 18, no. 4: 399-415.

Herrmann, Andreas, Torsten Tomczak, and Rene Befurt. 2006. "Determinants of Radical Product Innovations." *European Journal of Innovation Management* 9, no. 1: 20–43.

Jantz, Ronald C. 2013. "Incremental and Radical Innovations—Survey," May 20, doi:10.7282/T37D2S88.

Kaplan, Robert S. 2001. "Strategic Performance Measurement and Management in Nonprofit Organizations." *Nonprofit Management and Leadership* 11, no. 3 (Spring): 353–70.

Matthews, Joseph R. 2011. "Assessing Organizational Effectiveness: The Role of Performance Measures." *Library Quarterly* 81, no. 1 (January): 83–110. doi:10.1086/657447.

Mitchell, George E. 2012. "The Construct of Organizational Effectiveness: Perspectives from Leaders of International Nonprofits." *Nonprofit and Voluntary Sector Quarterly* 42, no. 2: 324–45.

Moon, M. Jae, and Peter deLeon. 2001. "Municipal Reinvention: Managerial Values and Diffusion among Municipalities." *Journal of Public Administration Research and Theory* 11, no. 3: 327–51.

Neal, James G. 2001. "The Entrepreneurial Imperative: Advancing from Incremental to Radical Change." *portal: Libraries and the Academy* 1, no. 1 (January): 1–13. doi: 10.7916/D8CZ358W.

O'Reilly III, Charles A., J. Bruce Harreld, and Michael L. Tushman. 2009. "Organizational Ambidexterity: IBM and Emerging Business Opportunities." *California Management Review* 51, no. 4 (August): 75–99.

Rivera, Mark D., Gregory Streib, and Katherine G. Willoughby. 2000. "Reinventing Government in Council-Manager Cities: Examining the Role of City Managers." *Public Performance and Management Review* 24, no. 2 (December): 121–32.

Robertson, Mark. 2015. "Perceptions of Canadian Provosts on the Institutional Role of Academic Libraries." *College and Research Libraries* 76, no. 4 (May): 490-511.

Salge, Torsten Oliver, and Antonio Vera. 2012. "Benefiting from Public Sector Innovation: The Moderating Role of Customer and Learning Orientation." *Public Administration Review* 72, no. 4 (July/August): 550–60.

Schneider, Benjamin, Arthur P. Brief, and Richard A. Guzzo. 1996. "Creating a Climate and Culture for Sustainable Organizational Change." *Organizational Dynamics* 24, no. 4 (Spring): 7–19. doi:10.1016/S0090-2616(96)90010-8.

Shera, Jesse Hauk. 1971. *"The Compleat Librarian" and Other Essays*. Cleveland, OH: The Press of Case Western Reserve University.

Chapter 12

The Innovative Library:
The Vision and the Transformation

WE HAVE APPLIED INNOVATION theory and concepts to understand how the research library innovates. The results, based on responses from library leaders, have shown that a more integrated leadership team with a strategy that embraces flexibility and a transparent decision process will be better able to address and resolve the conflicts that emerge from an innovative culture. As an unexpected result, libraries in this study with leadership teams in different age groups and long-tenured were able to innovate without the negative impact suggested by published theories. Based on recent theory and research, we posited that management innovations must precede and facilitate the technical innovation in order to achieve a successful implementation. In perhaps the most intuitive finding, the underlying data demonstrated that the library director's orientation toward risk taking and support of exploratory work was positively related to the innovation performance of the library.

Future Research

The findings in this study can help managers in the work of developing a more innovative culture. However, there are other promising research initiatives that can provide insights into how the research library innovates.

Research

A quantitative approach and a regression model do not provide a complete picture of innovation in institutional nonprofits. This study demonstrated that approximately 50 percent of the variance in innovation performance is explained by five factors. What other factors are affecting innovation in the research library? A qualitative case study including interviews of research library leaders will likely reveal interesting aspects of library culture, the singular leader, and the institutional environment. For future research, one might create a sample of the most innovative and least innovative libraries and conduct interviews with library leaders and managers. Analysis of the responses can provide explanations for what works and doesn't work in developing a more creative culture.

The question of the long-term survival of the research library is a perplexing one. The growing dissonance between the rapid advancement of technology and the research library's ability to adapt quickly will be difficult to overcome. One can imagine the library continuing at a rather slow rate of transformation by continuing to implement incremental innovations. Another scenario suggests the library becomes primarily a symbolic presence on the campus where most resources are available electronically and the library serves as a study and social gathering space for students. A third view is that libraries will successfully create and implement radical new service innovations.

Some organizational theorists have posed the question "Why can't an institution thrive by conducting only incremental innovations?" Based on past experience and observation, one can conclude that research libraries might survive quite nicely for many years. However, this incremental trajectory can be particularly insidious in an institution with aging professionals and inadequate performance indicators, allowing leaders to rationalize a traditional strategy of supporting the status quo. Understanding the impact of a continued incremental approach would help practitioners devise appropriate actions to avoid what might be considered a "failed" research library.

This study has focused on the factors that affect technical innovations as opposed to administrative innovations. From a methodological point of view, administrative innovations are sometimes more difficult to identify and vary widely across different libraries. Administrative innovations such as Total Quality Management (TQM) are frequently implemented piecemeal, and it is difficult to discern when the total innovation has been completed (Ravichandran 2000). Within an institutional nonprofit, the drivers for technical and administrative innovations are likely to be quite different. In their study of public libraries, Damanpour, Szabat, and Evan

(1989) highlighted the importance to organizational performance of a balanced rate of adoption for both administrative and technical innovations. Scholars continue to differ on which type of innovation originates first in the diffusion process. Some have argued that technical innovations precede administrative innovations in time. For example, one might expect a radical innovation to force major change in the organization, a situation that can prompt leaders to introduce new administrative practices. What might be the temporal order in a more ambidextrous organization in which managers create both incremental and radical innovations? Understanding the factors that drive administrative innovations can provide a more complete picture of how research libraries innovate and also provide library leaders with key insights as to appropriate actions to be taken.

Further research is required to understand the relationship between the research library and the university. In the development of new services, the library becomes a partner and collaborator with other units in the university. Some institutions may offer a more supportive and receptive climate to these innovations emanating from the library. How does the innovative university affect the research library and vice versa? Can an innovative research library help the university become more innovative? Answering these questions might lead to a better understanding of the role of the research library in the 21st century university.

Innovation Enablers

Where does the innovation process start? Our examination of innovation in libraries began with a discussion of the diffusion process (figure 3.1), suggesting that ideas, new knowledge, and technological advancements can jump-start the diffusion process. If we have ideas flowing into the organization, how is one to determine which ideas to act upon?

Process Needs

How are priorities for new work established in the library? Given the different stakeholders and the many possibilities for new services, a process for determining and communicating priorities could serve as a significant enabler. Obviously, in this more complex world, a single priority queue does not meet the needs of an organization with a diverse portfolio of services. If work priorities are established for each major service offering, the result can be an effective management tool and also one that enables leadership to clearly communicate priorities to organizational members. This priority process can complement the innovation portfolio and become part of the transition to more autonomous units for each library service and a decentralized organizational structure.

Incongruities

Identifying trends and incongruities, both within and external to the library, is becoming increasingly important. In the examination of reference transactions in ARL libraries, Folk (2015) reported a 30 percent decrease from 2006 to 2010, suggesting an opportunity was emerging for a change in this traditional service.

Are research libraries still in the book business? In a partnership with Emory University, Georgia Tech's library will move 95% of their books to a cold storage facility. This action is part of the vision and transformation of the library to a service organization with a large online presence, motivated in part by a dramatic decline in book circulation. According to Catherine L. Murray-Rust, dean of libraries, the objective is to change how people think of the research library in the 21st century (Straumsheim 2015).

A prediction. Investment in software applications and related platforms along with the associated competencies and methods will be a major part of the future research library. Earlier in this study, we stressed the importance of developing ideas and new knowledge, human resources that become the enablers of major new innovations, many of which will originate in software applications. Armour (2015) suggests that we think of software as a knowledge storage medium; when the knowledge is incomplete we have unreliable software that is difficult to use. A software bug is simply a lack of knowledge. Software becomes an extension of and a place where we store our thinking. The end user benefits from the stored knowledge that is embedded in the software. Increasingly, user requirements for new library services will originate in documents, but ultimately this knowledge is stored in and will have to be maintained in software libraries.

Software competencies go beyond programming skills and include core concepts and knowledge of software architecture, operating systems, and associated methods for producing high-quality software. Software applications and the embedded algorithms are a key to transferring potential library applications from external sources and customizing them to work in a research university environment. These software entities are emerging for virtually every library application including reference, bibliographic instruction, institutional repositories, science data, publishing, and emerging new possibilities.

As one incongruity, artificial intelligence promises to have an impact on the library, perhaps even more significant that the Internet and mobile computing. One can conceive of an adaptive learning application that analyzes or organizes unstructured data. Similar to emerging innovations in journalism, librarians and their clients might use data mining and classification to uncover trends that are impossible to create manually (Kirkpatrick 2015). Recently researchers have prototyped what they call a "metro map," which enables users to deal with the data deluge by providing an automatic method for extracting structured knowledge from a variety of resources (Shahaf et al. 2015). The metro map becomes a valuable literature exploration tool. For example, a PhD student might want to understand the important topics and relationships in an emerging field of study before selecting a dissertation topic. The metro approach can be applied to books, journal articles, and a variety of other text-based resources.

A Sense of Urgency

Martell (2000) was very articulate in suggesting that libraries will need to create new services in the 21st century that were unthinkable in the 20th century. However, Martell's perspective did not impart a sense of urgency. As noted earlier, Harvard University officials have warned of the rapid and disorienting change that is confronting universities (Martin 2012). Libraries have also witnessed their inability to adapt quickly to the rapidly changing technological environment. Research libraries are gradually edging into services for scholarly publishing and providing repositories for science data. Although these initiatives represent important new services, they raise questions regarding the rate of transformation and the nature of innovations, suggesting that the introduction of major change in the library will need to be accelerated. As part of the library transformation, one of the most significant management innovations will focus on this rate of change where the internal organizational rate of change will need to approximate the rate of change in the external environment (Volberda and van den Bosch 2005).

Concluding Observations

This study has highlighted the importance of the integrated leadership team. These leaders have a most complex task in developing responses to a dynamic environment and dealing with the day-to-day administrative challenges. Stimuli from the external environment are often vague and conflicting, resulting in a decision-making atmosphere that is ambiguous and often confusing. The importance of the singular leader is demonstrated in both theory and the empirical results of this study. In addition to architecting the organizational life of the library, this leader can facilitate change by becoming an idea champion, establishing the conditions to support innovation, and rewarding individual creative effort. The singular leader, however, without the contributions of the integrated team will not be able to create an innovative culture that is sustainable over time and largely independent of who is at the helm of the organization.

Even with an integrated senior team and a more ambidextrous orientation, we are still left with an important question: what kind of organization is the research library? As leaders have called for the transformation of the library, it is still unclear as to what this transformation will entail. The transformation will likely be quite different for each research library where differing strategies focus on revenue-generating services or on a more tightly bound collaborative network of like-minded institutions. We can imagine a future in which there is much more variation in how each library chooses to navigate the transformation. The resulting library culture becomes a hybrid, maintaining traditional values and ethics while also adopting selected business practices for balanced innovation and tracking organizational performance.

A vision that is explicit and attainable is needed in order to guide the transformation, rather than taking incremental and uncertain steps in an unknown direction. The vision should challenge the status quo and energize action in organizational members. Without this vision, it is unclear how the library can move from its current position to a desired future state. In all likelihood, changes in the vision and strategy of the library will have to come first in order to provide a guiding framework for change. And, in the final analysis, these changes probably suggest a change in the leaders themselves.

For concluding thoughts, it is appropriate to return to the comments of two library scholars who bracket the past half-century of library literature. Their writings reveal a common refrain about how the library profession can change by placing the focus on knowledge rather than information exchange. In his many philosophical writings, Jesse Shera has emphasized the importance of reflection. He has succinctly stated the professional dilemma: "The first responsibility of a profession is to know itself, which means, first, knowing what a profession is; second knowing what kind of a profession it is; and third, knowing what differentiates it from all other professions" (Shera 1965, 162). Shera (1965, 15–16) claims that librarianship needs a new approach—an epistemological discipline that develops a body of knowledge about knowledge.

More recently, John Budd offers a framework for understanding and debating difficult problems regarding the use of technology, the library building, and the future of librarianship—all with an emphasis on reflection and ethical implications. He voices optimism in the following quote: "If there is any grounding for doubting the future of LIS, and particularly of librarianship, it would be any betrayal of the commitment to knowledge" (Budd 2001, 328). These thoughts are not prescriptive, but they suggest a reorientation in thinking and the benefit of occasionally distancing ourselves from the details of management in order to think more philosophically about the library profession.

References

Armour, Phillip G. 2015. "The Business of Software: Thinking Thoughts." *Communications of the ACM* 58, no. 10 (October): 32–34.

Budd, John M. 2001. *Knowledge and Knowing in Library and Information Science*. Lanham, MD: Scarecrow Press.

Damanpour, Fariborz, Kathryn A. Szabat, and William M. Evan. 1989. "The Relationship between Types of Innovation and Organizational Performance." *Journal of Management Studies* 26, no. 6 (November): 587–601.

Folk, Amanda L. 2015. "Access or Awareness? Identifying Relationships between Reference and Other Dimensions of Public Services." Presentation, ACRL Conference, Portland, OR, March 25–28. http://www.ala.org/acrl/sites/ala.org.acrl/files/content/conferences/confsandpreconfs/2015/Folk_Access.pdf.

Kirkpatrick, Keith 2015. "Putting the Data Science into Journalism" *Communications of the ACM* 58, no. 5: 15–17. doi:10.1145/2742484.

Martell, Charles. 2000. "The Disembodied Librarian in the Digital Age." *College and Research Libraries* 61, no. 1 (January): 10–28. doi:10.5860/crl.61.1.10.

Martin, Andrew. 2012. "Building a Showcase Campus, Using an I.O.U." *New York Times*, December 13, A1, B4.

Ravichandran, T. 2000. "Swiftness and Intensity of Administrative Innovation Adoption: An Empirical Study of TQM in Information Systems." *Decision Sciences* 31, no. 3 (September): 691–724.

Shahaf, Dafna, Carlos Guestrin, Eric Horvitz, and Jure Leskovec. 2015. "Information Cartography." *Communications of the ACM* 58, no. 11: 62–73.

Shera, Jesse Hauk. 1965. *Libraries and the Organization of Knowledge*. Hamden, CT: Archon Books.

Straumsheim, Carl. 2015. "Out of the Stacks." *Inside Higher Ed,* January 13. https://www.insidehighered.com/news/2016/01/13/georgia-tech-emory-university-begin-work-tie-libraries-together.

Volberda, H. W., and F. A. J. van den Bosch. 2005. "Why Management Matters Most. *European Business Forum,* no. 22: 36–40. http://hdl.handle.net/1765/10939.

Appendix A

The 32 Research Library Innovations

The Final Innovations Used in the Survey (*N* = 32)

The table below provides a brief description of each innovation used in the survey distributed to ARL library leadership teams. The innovations were evaluated and selected by a focus group consisting of both library professionals and LIS faculty. At the time of the survey (2012), each innovation had been implemented by at least one ARL library. The table also shows the innovation continuum by including radical and incremental innovations and those innovations that lie between the incremental and radical—the midrange innovations.

Innovation Number	Radical	Incremental	Midrange
1	Provision of a service to publish e-journals	The sharing of a technology platform (e.g., an OPAC or institutional repository) with another library	A collaboration with another library to share collection development
2	The provision of a GIS (Geographic Information System) service to students and faculty, including access to GIS software, training, and consultation	A device and associated service to allow students and faculty to check out their own book	A service for the submission, access, and preservation of ETDs (electronic theses and dissertations)

Innovation Number	Radical	Incremental	Midrange
3	Provision of a service to faculty and students for multimedia production including instruction, software, and equipment platforms to support multimedia creation and publication	The use of live chat and instant messaging for reference service	The offering of a Wi-Fi service to the local community (i.e., not members of the university community)
4	Provision of a science data service including archiving, preservation, and access to research data and liaison support to researchers	Installation of a coffee bar/restaurant/café in the library	The provision of digital exhibits for special collections or other unique materials that are owned by the library
5	Replacement of stack book storage and preservation with digital book storage and digital preservation	Provision of a service to inexpensively print, bind, and trim bookstore-quality paperbacks from digital book files that are out of copyright	The embedding of library liaisons with students and the instructor in course management systems
6	Made the transition to a bookless (i.e., no print books) library for certain disciplines (e.g., engineering)	Provision of a mobile device lending service (laptop, netbook, iPad, etc.)	Provision of federated searching across the library OPAC, the institutional repository, and other open repositories
7	Implemented a liaison service to provide assistance to faculty researchers for managing their copyrights, e.g., in order to fulfill article deposit requirements from the National Institutes of Health and other institutions	Use of RSS feeds (or similar technology) to provide library news and event descriptions to library patrons	Use of digital object identifiers (e.g., DOIs or Handles) to create long-term, stable links to digital resources that are locally owned or created (digitized resources, dissertations, special collections, etc.)

Innovation Number	Radical	Incremental	Midrange
8	The creation of an institutional repository to contain the research output of the university (e.g., faculty research, dissertations, etc.)	Delivery of bibliographic instruction using online tutorials	Provision of mobile access to the library website and online catalog
9	Provided a dynamic mapping application for the OPAC to provide patrons directional information to find a shelved item	Reconfiguration of physical space and redesigned services to provide information or learning commons (a central location for workstations, information resources, and librarian assistance)	Creation of a website or portal for faculty that provides services and assistance for article deposit into the institution's repository
10		A service to digitize and provide online access to historic, print course catalogs	The development of a flexible bibliographic instruction course structure that gives students the option of attending sessions in the classroom, participating online, or doing both
11		Outsourced reference service to another organization (e.g., another library, nonprofit, or a commercial organization)	Implementation of faceted browsing for the library OPAC
12		Provided for the digitization and access to historic university yearbooks	

Appendix B

Independent and Control Variables

Independent Variables

Behavioral Integration

Simsek and colleagues (2005) extended Hambrick's (1994)model of behavioral integration by developing a measure of the construct and demonstrating empirical support. Simsek's scale was used in the ARL study survey in which university library leaders responded to three questions for each behavioral integration factor.[30]

Ambidextrous Orientation

Lubatkin and colleagues (2006) extended He and Wong's (2004) measures for exploratory and exploitative orientations, resulting in a six-item scale for each concept. This scale has been adapted for research libraries. Sample questions for exploratory behavior include: (*a*) the library looks for technological ideas by thinking "outside the box" and (*b*) the library creates products or services that are innovative. Sample questions for exploitative behavior include: (*a*) the library commits to improve quality and lower costs and (*b*) the library continuously improves the reliability of its products and services.[31] Given the two dimensions of an ambidextrous orientation, various researchers have constructed measures by subtracting, multiplying, or adding the scores for exploration and exploitation (Gibson and Birkenshaw 2004; He and Wong 2004; Jansen et al. 2009). In this study, the additive approach was used. The theoretical rationale for this decision is that the additive score provides insight into the commitment to both exploration and exploitation.

---

[30] See Jantz 2013, questions 1–9.

[31] See Jantz 2013, questions 21–32.

Structural Differentiation

From the scale developed by Jansen and colleagues (2009), five questions were used to create a variable that characterizes the extent of *structural differentiation* within the library.[32] For example, one of the questions asks if the library has different units for exploratory and production activities. The resulting scale captures the extent to which leaders have partitioned their organization into separate units. For each of the scale items, a team score is computed as an average of the scores for each individual respondent. To develop an organizational score that represents the extent of structural differentiation, the mean team scores for the scale items are averaged, resulting in a final score for structural differentiation.

Uncertainty of the External Environment

In accordance with Milliken (1987) and Waldman and colleagues (2001), *environmental uncertainty* was constructed as a perception by leaders of the university library. A six-item scale, adapted from Khandwalla (1976) and Koberg (1987) is used to measure environmental uncertainty.[33] Four items were used from this scale that uniquely captures the respondent's ability to predict various aspects of the library external environment. For each item, a team score is computed as an average of the scores for each individual respondent. To develop an organizational score that represents the team's perception of the external environment, the mean team scores for each scale item are averaged, resulting in a final score for the research library.

Control Variables

In this study, certain variables can lead to alternative explanations or have an overriding effect on the dependent variable. To understand these effects, two control variables—organization size and type of institution (public or private)—were included in the research model.

Organization Size

Larger libraries typically have more slack resources that can be applied

---

[32] See Jantz 2013, questions 10–14.

[33] See Jantz 2013, questions 15-20.

to major new initiatives. This imbalance can possibly obscure the effects of the major constructs. As shown in figure 4.2, organizational size will be considered a control. There are several different approaches for operationalizing the *size* variable. A personnel measure works best for a labor-intensive service organization whereas a volume measure is more appropriate for a manufacturing organization. In this study, total personnel (FTE) was used for the size variable and was taken from the annual Association of Research Libraries statistics for the academic year 2010–2011 (ARL 2011).

Type of Institution

For *type of institution* a variable was created where a public institution is assigned the value of 1 and a private institution is assigned the value of 0.

References

ARL (Association of Research Libraries). 2011. *ARL Statistics 2010–2011.* http://publications.arl.org/ARL-Statistics-2010-2011.

Gibson, Cristina B., and Julian Birkinshaw. 2004. "The Antecedents, Consequences, and Mediating Role of Organizational Ambidexterity." *Academy of Management Journal* 47, no. 2 (April): 209–26.

Hambrick, Donald C. 1994. "Top Management Groups: A Conceptual Integration and Reconsideration of the 'Team' Label." In *Research in Organizational Behavior,* vol. 16, edited by Barry M. Staw and Larry L. Cummings, 171–213. Greenwich, CT: JAI Press.

He, Zi-Lin, and Poh-Kam Wong. 2004. "Exploration vs. Exploitation: An Empirical Test of the Ambidexterity Hypothesis." *Organization Science* 15, no. 4 (July/August): 481–94.

Jansen, Justin J. P., Michiel P. Tempelaar, Frans A. J. van den Bosch, and Henk W. Volberda. 2009. "Structural Differentiation and Ambidexterity: The Mediating Role of Integration Mechanisms." *Organization Science* 20, no. 4: 797–811.

Jantz, Ronald C. 2013. "Incremental and Radical Innovations—Survey," May 20, doi:10.7282/T37D2S88.

Khandwalla, Pradip N. 1976. *The Design of Organizations.* New York: Harcourt Brace Jovanovich.

Koberg, Christine S. 1987. "Resource Scarcity, Environmental Uncertainty, and Adaptive Organizational Behavior." *Academy of Management Journal* 30, no. 4 (December): 798–807.

Lubatkin, Michael H., Zeki Simsek, Yan Ling, and John F. Veiga. 2006. "Ambidexterity and Performance in Small- to Medium-Sized Firms: The Pivotal Role of Top Management Team Behavioral Integration." *Journal of Management* 32, no. 5 (October): 646–72.

Milliken, Frances J. 1987. "Three Types of Perceived Uncertainty about the Environment: State, Effect and Response Uncertainty." *Academy of Management Review* 12, no. 1 (January): 133–43.

Simsek, Zeki, John F. Veiga, Michael H. Lubatkin, and Richard N. Dino. 2005. "Modeling the Multilevel Determinants of Top Management Team Behavioral Integration." *Academy of Management Journal* 48, no. 1 (February): 69–84.

Waldman, David A., Gabriel G. Ramirez, Robert J. House, and Phanish Puranam. 2001. "Does Leadership Matter? CEO Leadership Attributes and Profitability under Conditions of Perceived Environmental Uncertainty." *Academy of Management Journal* 44, no. 1 (February): 134–43.

Appendix C

Correlations of 17 Variables with Innovation Performance

	Var	1	2	3	4	5	6	7	8	9	10	11	12	13	14	15	15	17	18
IP	1	1.0																	
BI	2	.33[a]	1.0																
DA	3	.42[a]	.38[a]	1.0															
LDR	4	.24[b]	.26[b]	-.09	1.0														
AO	5	.42[a]	.63[a]	.36[a]	.54[a]	1.0													
AOB	6	-.36[a]	-.17	-.13	-.50[a]	-.41[a]	1.0												
SZ	7	.35[b]	.30[b]	-.07	.19	.15	-.19	1.0											
STR	8	-.22	-.08	-.33[b]	.17	.05	-.03	.12	1.0										
STF	9	.08	.09	.07	-.28	-.10	.27[b]	.14	-.04	1.0									
AFL	10	.00	-.07	-.23	.06	-.09	-.03	.46[a]	.13	.17	1.0								
ENM	11	.22	-.03	.02	-.14	-.14	-.12	.31[b]	.03	.33[b]	.10	1.0							
ENU	12	.11	-.23	.21	-.20	-.10	0.0	-.10	.06	-.05	.03	.19	1.0						
AGE	13	.03	.12	.22	-.13	.06	.08	-.14	-.09	-.06	-.20	0.0	-.09	1.0					
TEN	14	-.02	.26	.22	-.13	-.02	.22	-.12	.01	.20	-.27	.13	-.15	.66[a]	1.0				
TNP	15	-.04	.23	.03	.08	.20	-.02	-.30[b]	-.05	-.04	-.28[b]	-.21	-.14	.19	.21	1.0			
EDL	16	-.10	0.0	-.02	-.25	-.08	.18	-.07	.06	-.23	.03	-.22	.25	-.08	-.08	.03	1.0		
EDD	17	-.11	-.21	-.13	.13	-.10	.02	.11	.23	.01	-.29[b]	-.23	.17	-.24	-.13	-.13	.14	1.0	
EDS	18	-.08	.01	-.01	.29[b]	.08	-.23	.09	.10	-.10	.19	-.01	.16	-.22	-.23	-.28[b]	-.04	.60[a]	1.0

[a]Significant (2-tailed) at .01 level, [b]Significant at .05 level

Key to Variables: IP=Innovation performance, BI=Behavioral integration, DA=Decision awareness, LDR=Singular leader attitude, AO=Ambidextrous orientation, AOB=Ambidexterity (balance), SZ=Organizational size, STR=Structural differentiation, STF=Staff/professional profile, AFL=Affluence, ENM=Environmental munificence, ENU=Environmental uncertainty, AGE=TMT age, TEN=Professional tenure, TNP=Tenure in position, EDL=TMT level of education, EDD=TMT educational diversity, EDS=TMT educational diversity (science).

Appendix D

Means and Standard Deviations

Means and Standard Deviations for all Variables (*N* = 50)

Variable Number	Variable Label	Mean	Standard Deviation
1	Innovation performance	40.88	13.02
2	Behavioral integration	6.44	0.97
3	Decision awareness	61.43	11.56
4	Singular leader attitude	6.98	1.09
5	Ambidexterity	13.62	1.73
6	Ambidexterity (balance)	0.91	0.64
7	Organizational size	312.18	178.73
8	Structural differentiation	5.36	0.84
9	Staff/professional profile	15.19	15.01
10	Affluence (expense per student)	1250.70	902.14
11	Environmental munificence (change in expenditures)	36.50	21.75
12	Environmental uncertainty (predictability)	4.47	0.72
13	TMT age	55.52	4.13
14	TMT professional tenure	25.06	6.1
15	TMT tenure in position	7.33	4.30
16	Leader level of education	3.18	1.60
17	TMT educational diversity	1.98	0.62
18	TMT educational diversity (science)	0.56	0.71

Appendix E

Statistical Tests for Nonresponse Bias
Size and Region

FOR THE SAMPLE OF 50 libraries, potential nonresponse bias was assessed by determining if there was any significant difference in either the size of the library or the geographical region between participating and nonparticipating libraries. For size, an independent samples t-test was performed to assess whether the mean size of libraries participating in the innovation study differed significantly from the libraries that did not participate. The null hypothesis (H_0) for Levene's test is the two populations—participants and nonparticipants—have equal variance. The assumption of homogeneity of variance was assessed using the Levene test, $F = 3.52, p = .064$; this indicated no significant violation of the equal variance assumption. Therefore, the pooled variances version of the t-test was used. The means of the size variable for participants and nonparticipants did not differ significantly, $t(97) = 1.77, p = .08$, two-tailed. The mean for participants $(M = 320.23, SD = 181.05)$ was about 54.44 larger than the mean for nonparticipants $(M = 265.79, SD = 122.55)$. Therefore, the null hypothesis is not rejected.

The Wilcoxon Rank-Sum test is a nonparametric alternative to the two sample t-test. In this study, we wanted to test the hypothesis that the distribution of geographical regions among the library participants is the same as the distribution in the nonparticipating libraries. The null hypothesis (H_0) is that the mean ranks for the participants and the nonparticipants are equal. The Wilcoxon Rank-Sum test indicated no significant difference between these two groups, $W(n1 = 51, n2 = 48) = 2569.0, p = .826$ (two tailed). Therefore, the null hypothesis cannot be rejected. From both the Levene and Wilcoxon tests, it can be reasonably assumed that there is no nonresponse bias.

Index